Oregon's
Best Coastal Beaches

A Quick-Reference Guide

by
Dick Trout

©2005 Dick Trout

ALL RIGHTS RESERVED. No part of this book may be reproduced in any
means without the written consent of the Publisher, except in the case of brief
excerpts in critical reviews and articles.

Published in 2005 by
Frank Amato Publications, Inc.
PO Box 82112
Portland, Oregon 97282
(503) 653-8108
www.amatobooks.com

Softbound ISBN: 1-57188-364-9 • Softbound UPC: 0-81127-00198-9

All photographs taken by the author unless otherwise noted.
Book Design: Dick Trout
Cover Design: Tony Amato

Printed in Hong Kong

1 3 5 7 9 10 8 6 4 2

Table of Contents

Table of Contents (Cont'd)

Introduction

This book will help you find beaches on the Oregon coast that have what you are looking for in the way of facilities, amenities and activities for any particular trip to the beach from points inland.

These pages do suggest some activities, such as a visit to a lighthouse, but do not really focus on general sightseeing. Mostly the book's purpose is to help you find the good beaches – good sand, sun (maybe), interesting phenomena and useful amenities - so you know what to expect when you get there. If you are looking for a beach to have a picnic, you want to know which ones have tables and perhaps fresh water; if you've got the kids along then restrooms are quite important.

Feel like watching surfers brave the waves, or doing some horseback riding on the sand? This book tells you where to go for these things. Looking for somewhere to take really interesting and scenic photographs? Miners Creek, for one, is exceptional for this. And this book is a reliable guide to many of the good trails that stretch your legs and test your stamina.

All the beaches shown in this book will provide you with a pleasant "day at the beach." Although Oregon has a bountiful supply of mostly excellent, scenic beaches there are a few poor ones and these have been omitted. Some have been too despoiled to be included, or are just too difficult to access for the average person or family.

How This Book Is Organized

One page is devoted to each beach. You'll find a landscape photo at the top of the page showing a typical, representative scene. An aerial photo that gives you a feel for the lay of the land near the beach is at the bottom of the page, along with a one-sentence description of just where it is in reference to either US Highway 101 or to the coastal town roads that provide access.

In the center of each page are the details for this beach in two tabular columns, plus some general information and helpful (or just interesting) remarks in a third column.

These Oregon beaches are arranged in sequential order from Fort Stevens State Park at the mouth of the Columbia River in the north to Crissey Field State Recreation Site right on the southern border with California. A general location arrow and map on each beach page lets you scan through a section of the coast quickly. To find a beach by name check the index at the back of the book which lists them all. Or, just use the locator maps on each page, and scan for the area that most interests you for planning your next trip.

How to read the Beach Pages

The aerial photos are on a scale covering about a two miles wide area; a few cover a larger area which show such landmarks as headlands or estuaries better. You'll probably find it easy to use to these aerials.

Here is what you'll find in the various columns:

Managed By (Mgd by): When there is no apparent manager, *OPRD* is shown since all beaches are under the ultimate authority of the Oregon Parks and Recreation Department. *State Parks* is used for designated State Parks, Waysides, etc.

Nearby access: Means the beach is within about 200 yards of parking, or such other things as the boat basin on the Chetco River in the case of Sport Haven.

Handicap access is not noted since this is so very subjective.

Vehicle access: Means there is parking where it's only a short walk to the beach.

Hiking/trails: Refers to maintained trails, not just walking along the beach or scrambling down the bluffs.

Information Center: Not all have a person in attendance.

Surfing 'yes': This term refers to both board and sail surfing and is noted wherever I've seen it or heard/read about it, or if it is listed on the Surfrider Foundation's web site (www.surfrider.org/oregon/), which records the prime spots. Surfing is done many other places, of course, as the mood and wave action strikes the surfers.

Whale watching: Locations noted are mostly from the OPRD Official Whale Watch Locations list.

Fees: More parks, places and viewpoints are being added to the fee list each year; be forewarned.

The stars: Most beaches are rated as three stars ★ ★ ★ ☆ ☆ and are excellent. Even the one and two stars beaches are worth a visit. Really poor ones, or those very difficult to get to are left out. Some places are omitted because they are on lakes with no direct access, e.g. Tugman and Floras Lake State Parks;

Loeb State Park is way too far from an ocean beach.

Day Use vs. Camping locations: Usually the emphasis is on the Day Use area, with the full-service campground only noted.

Horse camps: Primitive campsites and corrals are available in some parks.

Other General Information:

- Accesses within a city usually are not shown as they are just a way to the beach from the end of a street, but a couple of exceptions are made, such as Nye Beach in Newport.

- A few of the included places are only *Viewpoints* but have picnic tables, bathrooms, etc. and may well be worth a stop for you.

- On rare occasion an additional attraction is walking and hiking, not just being on a beach, e.g. Cape Sebastian SSV.

Oregon Parks Classifications

All Oregon beaches are administered by OPRD, but many immediately adjoining parks are provided and maintained by various counties, the USFS, the BLM or a city. Since all actual Oregon beaches management is under OPRD, this is what is shown if no other party is known to be responsible.

These classifications are being re-worked by OPRD (Oregon Parks and Recreation Department). Many that in the past were *Waysides* are now specified as SRS (see below), SNA, SP, etc. For the most part the original *Wayside* signs have been left in place for now.

State Park: An extensively scenic, outstanding natural setting for a variety of outdoor recreation.

State Recreation Area/Site (SRA/SRS): A location with facilities that provide access to a variety of recreational pursuits.

State Natural Area/Site (SNA/SNS): An outstanding natural resource that may offer opportunities to view unique plants and wildlife.

State Scenic Viewpoint/Corridor (SSV/SSC): A scenic highway corridor or roadside spot that offers an outstanding view of natural features.

State Wayside: A small, sometimes isolated parcel of roadside land with a parking area, picnic tables and usually restrooms.

Oregon State Parks Information Center: 1-800-551-6949.

Abbreviations

Army Corps – U.S. Army Corps of Engineers

BLM – U. S. Bureau of Land Management

NRA – National Recreation Area

ODNRA – Oregon Dunes National Recreation Area

ODOT – Oregon Department of Transportation

OHV/ORV – Off Highway or Off Road Vehicle

OPRD – Oregon Parks and Recreation Department

USFS – U. S. Forest Service

Oregon Coast Watch

Welcome to our beautiful beaches! In Oregon all beaches are open to every-one. This becomes especially noteworthy when you consider that only 5 percent of the recreational shore land in the United States is open and available to the public. "In California, only 90 miles out of 1,072 miles of coastline are publicly owned," observed Brian Booth, a past chairman of the Oregon Parks and Recreation Commission. "That will give you some idea of how unique Oregon is."

Oregon's 'Beach Bill' of 1967, was initially pushed by the ad hoc citizen group, Citizens to Save Oregon Beaches, which later became Oregon Shores Conservation Coalition, the parent of CoastWatch. This was a response to attempts to cordon off portions of the beach from the public -- illegal though it was even then. Governor Tom McCall entered the fray and thanks to his efforts the Bill was finally enacted by the Legislature, All of Oregon's 362 miles of coastline are now solidly protected from such encroachments.

Unfortunately there continue to be attempts to misuse and abuse the coast and especially the beaches. Individuals attempt construction or modifications to the landscape in ignorance or defiance of Oregon law. Sometimes, even county commissioners approve actions that are improper and harmful to the general public's use of coastal areas. Threats to the access of the dry sand ocean-front beaches are ongoing and these efforts must be met head-on. No action means a loss.

Oregon CoastWatch is an organization made up of dedicated volunteers who get to know one mile of coast very well. They visit 'their' mile at least four times a year -- once each season. Some, of course, walk their mile many more times during the year. With nearly 1,200 members today, each mile of Oregon's coast is thus monitored for anything of interest that may affect the coastal environment in that area.

This program is in its second decade, and it undertakes four kinds of activities that are organized and monitored by its members. A primary activity is the "Paul Revere function" — CoastWatchers spread the alarm when they discover an impact or violation such as oil on the beach, illegal rip-rapping or other shoreline protection structures, or when they come upon vehicles outside posted limits and other inappropriate actions.

The other three activities are information-gathering, acting as advocates before planning bodies in specific instances when public comment is appropriate, and educating others and themselves on developments up and down the coast that are affecting how the beaches are preserved, used and maintained.

Since volunteers do come and go, new folks to adopt a mile are always very welcome. Those interested may contact Philip Johnson at 605 SE 37th Ave., Portland, OR 97214, or go to *www.oregonshores.org*.

Fort Stevens State Park

		Nearby Beach Access		Rating:	

Mgd by: State Parks

Parking Lot : **many**

" roadside – no

Nearby Beach Access		Rating:
Pedestrian	yes	★ ★ ★ ★ ★
Vehicle	yes	
Boat	yes	3,763 acres

Drinking water	yes			Oregon's
Tables/benches	yes	Recreation		largest state
Restrooms	yes	Horse riding	yes	park. Great for
Camping	yes	Tidepooling	no	biking. Historic
Showers	yes	WhaleWatching	yes	military site.
Phone	yes	Surfing	yes	Swimming at
Info Center	yes	Bicycling	yes	Coffenbury
Fee	yes	Hiking/trails	yes	Lake. More!
[Peter Iredale shipwreck]		Boating	yes	

Astoria
Seaside
Tillamook
Lincoln City
Newport
Florence
Reedsport
Coos Bay
Bandon
Port Orford
Gold Beach
Brookings

Peter --> Iredale

<-- Coffenbury Lake

Warrenton

Columbia Beach -->

Aerial photo courtesy of U.S. Geological Survey, 27May94   **Width is approx. 2 miles**

Off US 101, 10 miles west of Astoria at the mouth of the Columbia River.

Sunset Beach

Mgd by: Clatsop Co.		Nearby Beach Access		Rating:
Parking Lot :	**small**	Pedestrian	**yes**	★ ★ ★ ☆ ☆
" roadside –	**yes**	Vehicle	**yes**	
		Boat	no	Driving on the
Drinking water	no			very wide
Tables/benches	no	Recreation		beach is
Restrooms	no	Horse riding	no	allowed here.
Camping	no	Tidepooling	no	It gets a lot of
Showers	no	WhaleWatching	no	use by the
Phone	no	Surfing	no	locals.
Info Center	no	Bicycling	no	
Fee	no	Hiking/trails	no	
[That's a jet ski you see]		Boating	no	

→ Astoria
Seaside
Tillamook
Lincoln City
Newport
Florence
Reedsport
Coos Bay
Bandon
Port Orford
Gold Beach
Brookings

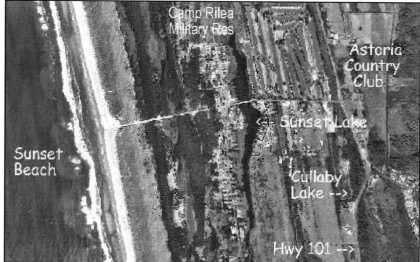

Aerial photo courtesy of U.S. Geological Survey, 27May94   **Width is approx. 2 miles**

Off US 101, 7 miles north of Seaside.

Del Rey Beach State Recreation Site

Mgd by: State Parks		Nearby Beach Access		Rating:	
Parking Lot :	**large**	Pedestrian	**yes**	★ ★ ★ ☆ ☆	
" roadside –	**yes**	Vehicle	**yes**		
		Boat	no	Driving on the	
Drinking water	no			very wide	
Tables/benches	no	Recreation		beach is	
Restrooms	no	Horse riding	**yes**	allowed here.	
Camping	no	Tidepooling	no	Popular with	
Showers	no	WhaleWatching	no	the locals.	
Phone	no	Surfing	**yes**		
Info Center	no	Bicycling	no		
Fee	no	Hiking/trails	no		
		Boating	no		

→ Astoria
Seaside

Tillamook
Lincoln City
Newport
Florence
Reedsport
Coos Bay
Bandon
Port Orford
Gold Beach
Brookings

Del Rey
Beach -->

Hwy 101 -->

Neacoxie
<-- Creek

golf
course

Aerial photo courtesy of U.S. Geological Survey, 27May94   **Width is approx. 2 miles**

Off US 101, 3½ miles north of Seaside.

3

Indian Beach - Ecola State Park

Mgd by: State Parks	Nearby Beach Access		Rating:	
Parking Lot: **medium**	Pedestrian	**yes**	★ ★ ★ ★ ★	Astoria
" roadside – no	Vehicle	**yes**		Seaside
	Boat	no	1,304 acres	Tillamook
Drinking water **yes**				Lincoln City
Tables/benches **yes**	Recreation		Hike-in	Newport
Restrooms **yes**	Horse riding	no	camping at	Florence
Camping **yes**	Tidepooling	**yes**	Indian Creek.	Reedsport
Showers no	WhaleWatching	no	Enjoy the trail	
Phone no	Surfing	**yes**	from the north	Coos Bay
Info Center no	Bicycling	no	around	Bandon
Fee **yes**	Hiking/trails	**yes**	Tillamook	Port Orford
[Tillamook Rock Lighthouse] Boating		no	Head to here.	Gold Beach
				Brookings

Aerial photo courtesy of U.S. Geological Survey, 27May94   **Width is approx. 2 miles**

Enter from north end of Cannon Beach, then north 1.8 miles on winding road.

Crescent Beach - Ecola State Park

		Nearby Beach Access		Rating:	
Mgd by:	State Parks	Pedestrian	yes	★ ★ ★ ★ ★	
Parking Lot :	large	Vehicle	no		
" roadside –	no	Boat	no	1,304 acres	
Drinking water	yes				
Tables/benches	yes	Recreation		"Terrible Tilly"	
Restrooms	yes	Horse riding	no	Lighthouse 1.2	
Camping	no	Tidepooling	yes	miles offshore.	
Showers	no	WhaleWatching	yes		
Phone	yes	Surfing	no	Exhilarating	
Info Center	no	Bicycling	no	view of coast	
Fee	yes	Hiking/trails	yes	and Haystack	
[Tillamook Rock Lighthouse] Boating			no	Rock.	

Astoria
Seaside
Tillamook
Lincoln City
Newport
Florence
Reedsport
Coos Bay
Bandon
Port Orford
Gold Beach
Brookings

Ecola Point→

Crescent Beach -->

Ecola State Park

Chapman Point -->

Chapman Beach -->

Aerial photo courtesy of U.S. Geological Survey, 27May94   ***Width is approx. 2 miles***

Enter from north end of Cannon Beach, then north 1.8 miles on winding road.

Cannon Beach

		Nearby Beach Access		Rating:	
Mgd by: Cannon Beach					Astoria
Parking Lot :	**large**	Pedestrian	**yes**	★★★☆☆	Seaside
" roadside –	**a few**	Vehicle	**yes**		Tillamook
		Boat	no	235 ft. high	Lincoln City
Drinking water	**yes**			Haystack Rock	Newport
Tables/benches	**yes**	Recreation		just offshore.	
Restrooms	**yes**	Horse riding	**yes**	Famous sand-	Florence
Camping	no	Tidepooling	**yes**	castle contest	Reedsport
Showers	no	WhaleWatching	no	in late spring.	Coos Bay
Phone	**yes**	Surfing	no	You can walk	Bandon
Info Center	no	Bicycling	**yes**	on the beach	Port Orford
Fee	no	Hiking/trails	no	to Arch Rock.	Gold Beach
[Artsy, often crowded town]		Boating	no	Kite flying.	Brookings

Aerial photo courtesy of U.S. Geological Survey, 27May94   ***Width is approx. 2 miles***

Off US 101, on south side of Tillamook Head. Several beach access points.

6

Tolovana Beach State Recreation Site

		Nearby Beach Access		Rating:	
Mgd by:	State Parks				
Parking Lot :	**large**	Pedestrian	**yes**	★ ★ ★ ☆ ☆	
" roadside –	no	Vehicle	**yes**		
		Boat	no	Nice beach in	
Drinking water	**yes**			a rather	
Tables/benches	**yes**	Recreation		crowded, built	
Restrooms	**yes**	Horse riding	no	up area with	
Camping	no	Tidepooling	no	many motels.	
Showers	no	WhaleWatching	no	Popular.	
Phone	**yes**	Surfing	no		
Info Center	**yes**	Bicycling	no		
Fee	no	Hiking/trails	no		
[Clean, well-kept beach]		Boating	no		

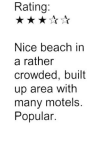

Astoria
Seaside
Tillamook
Lincoln City
Newport
Florence
Reedsport
Coos Bay
Bandon
Port Orford
Gold Beach
Brookings

Tolovana
Beach SRS -->

Tolovana
Park

<-- Hwy 101

Aerial photo courtesy of U.S. Geological Survey, 27May94   ***Width is approx. 2 miles***

Off US 101, one mile south of Cannon Beach.

Arcadia Beach State Recreation Site

Mgd by:	State Parks	
Parking Lot:	**medium**	
" roadside –	no	
Drinking water	no	
Tables/benches	**yes**	
Restrooms	**yes**	
Camping	no	
Showers	no	
Phone	no	
Info Center	no	
Fee	no	

Nearby Beach Access

Pedestrian	**yes**
Vehicle	**yes**
Boat	no

Recreation

Horse riding	no
Tidepooling	no
WhaleWatching	no
Surfing	no
Bicycling	no
Hiking/trails	no
Boating	no

Rating:
★ ★ ★ ☆ ☆

This very popular beach has a friendly feeling. Finding a parking place can be a problem.

Astoria
Seaside
Tillamook
Lincoln City
Newport
Florence
Reedsport
Coos Bay
Bandon
Port Orford
Gold Beach
Brookings

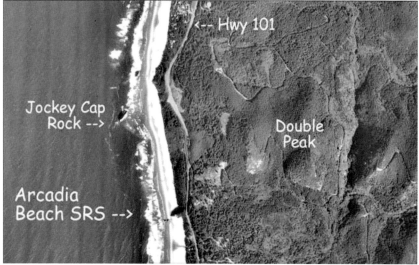

<-- Hwy 101

Jockey Cap
Rock -->

Double
Peak

Arcadia
Beach SRS -->

Aerial photo courtesy of U.S. Geological Survey, 27May94   **Width is approx. 2 miles**

Off US 101, 3 miles south of Cannon Beach.

Hug Point State Recreation Site

Mgd by: State Parks	Nearby Beach Access		Rating:
Parking Lot : **large**	Pedestrian	**yes**	★★★★☆
" roadside – no	Vehicle	**yes**	
	Boat	no	43 acres

Drinking water no
Tables/benches **yes**
Restrooms **yes**
Camping no
Showers no
Phone no
Info Center no
Fee no
[Natural caves]

Recreation
Horse riding no
Tidepooling no
WhaleWatching no
Surfing no
Bicycling no
Hiking/trails no
Boating no

A stage-coach road ran here around the point at low tide, when the beach was the coast highway.

Astoria
Seaside

Tillamook

Lincoln City
Newport

Florence

Reedsport

Coos Bay
Bandon
Port Orford

Gold Beach
Brookings

Arcadia Beach -->

Fall Creek

Hug Point
SRS -->

<-- Hug Point

<-- Hwy 101

Aerial photo courtesy of U.S. Geological Survey, 27May94   ***Width is approx. 2 miles***

Off US 101, 4 miles south of Cannon Beach.

Arch Cape – Oswald West State Park

		Nearby Beach Access		Rating:
Mgd by:	OPRD	Pedestrian	**yes**	★ ★ ☆ ☆ ☆
Parking Lot :	no	Vehicle	**yes**	
" roadside –	**a few**	Boat	no	Access is via
				Leech Lane,
Drinking water	no			just north of the
Tables/benches	no	Recreation		tunnel. You can
Restrooms	no	Horse riding	no	walk 1 mile
Camping	no	Tidepooling	no	north on the
Showers	no	WhaleWatching	no	beach to Hug
Phone	no	Surfing	no	Point, or all the
Info Center	no	Bicycling	no	way to Cannon
Fee	no	Hiking/trails	**yes**	Beach.
[Very residential area]		Boating	no	

Aerial photo courtesy of U.S. Geological Survey, 27May94 **Width is approx. 2 miles**

Off US 101, 6 miles south of Cannon Beach.

Cove Beach [Falcon Cove] – Oswald West State Park

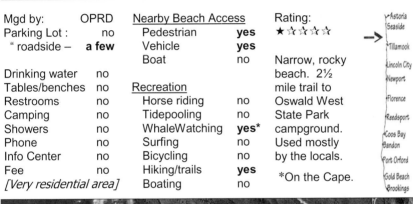

		Nearby Beach Access		Rating:
Mgd by:	OPRD	Pedestrian	**yes**	★ ☆ ☆ ☆ ☆
Parking Lot :	no	Vehicle	**yes**	
" roadside –	**a few**	Boat	no	Narrow, rocky
				beach. 2½
Drinking water	no			mile trail to
Tables/benches	no	Recreation		Oswald West
Restrooms	no	Horse riding	no	State Park
Camping	no	Tidepooling	no	campground.
Showers	no	WhaleWatching	**yes***	Used mostly
Phone	no	Surfing	no	by the locals.
Info Center	no	Bicycling	no	
Fee	no	Hiking/trails	**yes**	*On the Cape.
[Very residential area]		Boating	no	

→ Astoria, Seaside, Tillamook, Lincoln City, Newport, Florence, Reedsport, Coos Bay, Bandon, Port Orford, Gold Beach, Brookings

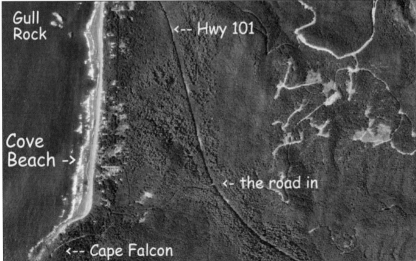

Gull Rock

<-- Hwy 101

Cove Beach ->

<-- the road in

<-- Cape Falcon

Aerial photo courtesy of U.S. Geological Survey, 27May94 **Width is approx. 2 miles**

Off US 101, 7 miles south of Cannon Beach, west down Falcon Cove Road.

Short Sand Beach – Oswald West State Park

Mgd by: State Parks	Nearby Beach Access		Rating:
Parking Lot : **several**	Pedestrian	**yes**	★ ★ ★ ★ ☆
" roadside – no	Vehicle	no	
	Boat	no	Oswald West
Drinking water **yes**			is 2,474 acres
Tables/benches **yes**	Recreation		
Restrooms **yes**	Horse riding	no	Wheelbarrows
Camping **yes**	Tidepooling	**yes**	for 30 walk-in
Showers no	WhaleWatching	**yes**	campsites. 15
Phone **yes**	Surfing	**yes**	minutes down
Info Center no	Bicycling	no	the trail to the
Fee no	Hiking/trails	**yes**	beach. Several
[Secluded beaches]	Boating	no	accesses.

↳Astoria
Seaside
→
↑Tillamook
Lincoln City
Newport
↑Florence
Reedsport
↓Coos Bay
Bandon
↑Port Orford
Gold Beach
↳Brookings

Aerial photo courtesy of U.S. Geological Survey, 27May94   ***Width is approx. 2 miles***

Off US 101, 9 miles south of Cannon Beach, 4 miles north of Manzanita.

Neahkahnie Beach at Manzanita

		Nearby Beach Access		Rating:	
Mgd by: City/County				★ ★ ★ ★ ☆	
Parking Lot :	no	Pedestrian	**yes**		
" roadside – **many**		Vehicle	**yes**		
		Boat	no	Watch whales	
Drinking water	no			from Hwy 101	
Tables/benches	no	Recreation		pull-outs on	
Restrooms	no	Horse riding	**yes**	700 ft. high	
Camping	no	Tidepooling	no	Neahkahnie	
Showers	no	WhaleWatching	**yes**	Mountain. A	
Phone	no	Surfing	**yes**	quiet, "hidden	
Info Center	no	Bicycling	**yes**	favorite" town.	
Fee	no	Hiking/trails	no		
[Use Ocean Ave. to beach] Boating			no		

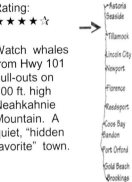

Aerial photo courtesy of U.S. Geological Survey, 27May94   **Width is approx. 2 miles**

Off US 101, 14 miles south of Cannon Beach.

Nehalem Bay State Park

		Nearby Beach Access		Rating:	
Mgd by:	State Parks			★ ★ ★ ★ ★	Astoria
Parking Lot :	**many**	Pedestrian	**yes**		Seaside
" roadside -	no	Vehicle	**yes**		Tillamook
		Boat	**yes**	890 acres	Lincoln City
Drinking water	**yes**				Newport
Tables/benches	**yes**	Recreation			
Restrooms	**yes**	Horse riding	**yes**	Sports, corrals,	Florence
Camping	**yes**	Tidepooling	no	fly-in camps.	Reedsport
Showers	**yes**	WhaleWatching	**yes**	6 miles of	Coos Bay
Phone	**yes**	Surfing	**yes**	beaches, a	Bandon
Info Center	**yes**	Bicycling	**yes**	2 mile spit.	Port Orford
Fee	**yes**	Hiking/trails	**yes**	Great place	Gold Beach
[Kayaking, 2,400 ft. airstrip]		Boating	**yes**	for picnics.	Brookings

Aerial photo courtesy of U.S. Geological Survey, 27May94   **Width is approx. 2 miles**

Entrance is off US 101, ½ mile south of Manzanita Junction.

14

Nedonna Beach

Mgd by: Army Corps		<u>Nearby Beach Access</u>		Rating:	Astoria
Parking Lot : **medium**		Pedestrian	**yes**	★ ★ ☆ ☆ ☆	Seaside
" roadside –	no	Vehicle	**yes**		Tillamook
		Boat	no	Turn west at	Lincoln City
Drinking water	no			Manhattan	Newport
Tables/benches	no	<u>Recreation</u>		Beach sign,	
Restrooms	no	Horse riding	no	then right 0.7	Florence
Camping	no	Tidepooling	no	mile to	Reedsport
Showers	no	WhaleWatching	no	Nehalem Bay	Coos Bay
Phone	no	Surfing	no	South Jetty.	Bandon
Info Center	no	Bicycling	no	Large drift-	Port Orford
Fee	no	Hiking/trails	no	wood area.	Gold Beach
[Very residential area]		Boating	no		Brookings

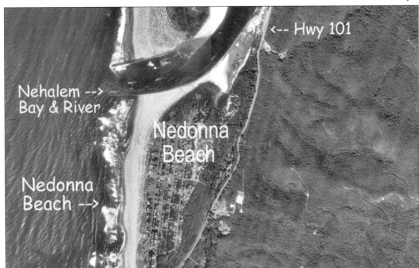

Aerial photo courtesy of U.S. Geological Survey, 27May94   ***Width is approx. 2 miles***

Off US 101, 3 miles north of Rockaway.

Manhattan Beach State Recreation Site

Mgd by: State Parks		Nearby Beach Access		Rating:
Parking Lot :	**large**	Pedestrian	**yes**	★ ★ ★ ☆ ☆
" roadside –	no	Vehicle	**yes**	
		Boat	no	Wind-shielded
Drinking water	**yes**			picnic sites.
Tables/benches	**yes**	Recreation		No view of the
Restrooms	**yes**	Horse riding	no	ocean from
Camping	no	Tidepooling	no	the picnic
Showers	no	WhaleWatching	no	area,
Phone	no	Surfing	no	but it's just a
Info Center	no	Bicycling	no	short walk to
Fee	no	Hiking/trails	no	the beach.
[Small, but has a park host]		Boating	no	

Astoria
Seaside
→ Tillamook
Lincoln City
Newport
Florence
Reedsport
Coos Bay
Bandon
Port Orford
Gold Beach
Brookings

Manhattan Beach -->   <-- Hwy 101

athletic field

<-- Crescent Lake

Manhattan Beach

<-- Lake Lytle

Aerial photo courtesy of U.S. Geological Survey, 27May94   **Width is approx. 2 miles**

Off US 101, 2 miles north of Rockaway Beach, 15 miles north of Tillamook.

Twin Rocks

		Nearby Beach Access		Rating:
Mgd by:	OPRD			★ ★ ★ ☆ ☆
Parking Lot :	no	Pedestrian	**yes**	
" roadside –	**a few**	Vehicle	**yes**	
		Boat	no	Literally tons of
Drinking water	no			driftwood here.
Tables/benches	no	Recreation		From Shand
Restrooms	no	Horse riding	no	Ave. turn right
Camping	no	Tidepooling	no	and go to the
Showers	no	WhaleWatching	no	end of the road
Phone	no	Surfing	no	for parking.
Info Center	no	Bicycling	no	
Fee	no	Hiking/trails	no	
[Very residential area]		Boating	no	

Astoria
Seaside

→ Tillamook

Lincoln City
Newport
Florence
Reedsport
Coos Bay
Bandon
Port Orford
Gold Beach
Brookings

Twin Rocks

Twin Rocks
Beach -->

<-- Spring Lake

Watseco Creek

<-- Hwy 101

Aerial photo courtesy of U.S. Geological Survey, 27May94   **Width is approx. 2 miles**

Off US 101, 12 miles north of Tillamook. Turn west at Shand Ave.

Barview Jetty County Park

		Nearby Beach Access		Rating:	
Mgd by: Tillamook Co.				★ ★ ★ ☆ ☆	Astoria
Parking Lot: **large**		Pedestrian	**yes**		Seaside
" roadside –	no	Vehicle	**yes**		
		Boat	no	Day use area	Tillamook
Drinking water	**yes**			has no	Lincoln City
Tables/benches	**yes**	Recreation		facilities.	Newport
Restrooms	**yes**	Horse riding	no	Campground	
Camping	**yes**	Tidepooling	no	has all	Florence
Showers	**yes**	WhaleWatching	no	amenities.	Reedsport
Phone	**yes**	Surfing	no	This is the	Coos Bay
Info Center	**yes**	Bicycling	no	entrance to	Bandon
Fee (Day use no) **yes**		Hiking/trails	**yes**	Tillamook Bay	Port Orford
[Popular with fishermen]		Boating	no		Gold Beach
					Brookings

<-- Hwy 101

<-- Smith Lake

Barview Jetty County Park -->

Barview

Aerial photo courtesy of U.S. Geological Survey, 27May94   ***Width is approx. 2 miles***

Off US 101, at the north end of Tillamook Bay.

Bay Ocean Spit

		Nearby Beach Access		Rating:	
Mgd by: Tillamook Co.				★ ★ ☆ ☆ ☆	
Parking Lot: **medium**		Pedestrian	**yes**		
" roadside –	**yes**	Vehicle	**yes**		
		Boat	no	On the dike road it's 1 mile to the end and parking. Then a 600 yard dry sand trail to the very nice beach.	
Drinking water	no				
Tables/benches	no	Recreation			
Restrooms	no	Horse riding	**yes**		
Camping	no	Tidepooling	no		
Showers	no	WhaleWatching	no		
Phone	no	Surfing	no		
Info Center	no	Bicycling	**yes**		
Fee	no	Hiking/trails	**yes**		
[Crabbing, clamming]		Boating	no		

Astoria
Seaside
→ Tillamook
Lincoln City
Newport
Florence
Reedsport
Coos Bay
Bandon
Port Orford
Gold Beach
Brookings

<-- parking

Netarts Bay

Bay Ocean or Netarts Spit

<-- dike

Cape Meares Lake

Pitcher Point

Aerial photo courtesy of U.S. Geological Survey, 27May94   **Width is approx. 2 miles**

From downtown Tillamook, it's 7 miles to the turnoff from 3 Capes Highway.

Cape Meares Beach

Mgd by:	OPRD	Nearby Beach Access		Rating:
Parking Lot::	**small**	Pedestrian	**yes**	★ ★ ☆ ☆ ☆
" roadside –	**a few**	Vehicle	**yes**	
		Boat	no	Two end-of-street beach access points. Parking is tight both places.
Drinking water	no			
Tables/benches	no	Recreation		
Restrooms	no	Horse riding	no	
Camping	no	Tidepooling	no	
Showers	no	WhaleWatching	no	
Phone	no	Surfing	no	
Info Center	no	Bicycling	no	
Fee	no	Hiking/trails	no	
[Very residential area]		Boating	no	

↘ Astoria
Seaside
➡ Tillamook
Lincoln City
Newport
Florence
Reedsport
Coos Bay
Bandon
Port Orford
Gold Beach
Brookings

Cape Meares Beach -->

Cape Meares

Three Capes Hwy -->

Cape Meares

Aerial photo courtesy of U.S. Geological Survey, 27May94   **Width is approx. 2 miles**

Off Three Capes Highway, due west of Tillamook, ¼ mile past Bay Ocean dike.

Cape Meares State Scenic Viewpoint

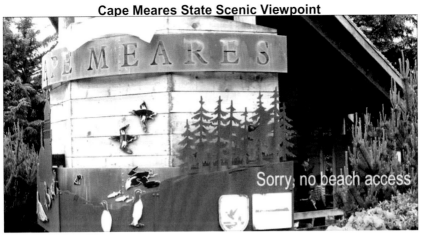

Sorry, no beach access

Mgd by:	State Parks	Nearby Beach Access		Rating:	Astoria
Parking Lot :	**large**	Pedestrian	no	★ ★ ★ ☆ ☆	Seaside
" roadside –	no	Vehicle	no		Tillamook
		Boat	no	233 acres	Lincoln City
Drinking water	**yes**				Newport
Tables/benches	**yes**	Recreation		Lighthouse	Florence
Restrooms	**yes**	Horse riding	no	open daily	Reedsport
Camping	no	Tidepooling	no	April thru	
Showers	no	WhaleWatching	**yes**	October.	Coos Bay
Phone	no	Surfing	no	"Octopus"	Bandon
Info Center	**yes**	Bicycling	no	Sitka Spruce.	Port Orford
Fee	no	Hiking/trails	**yes**	Also see *Short*	Gold Beach
[Cape Meares Lighthouse]		Boating	no	*Beach.*	Brookings

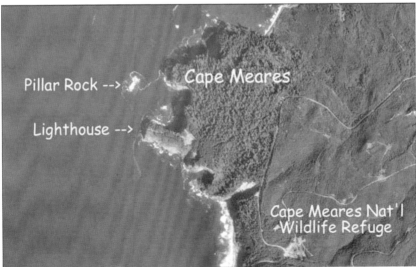

Pillar Rock -->

Cape Meares

Lighthouse -->

Cape Meares Nat'l Wildlife Refuge

Aerial photo courtesy of U.S. Geological Survey, 27May94   **Width is approx. 2 miles**

Off US 101, 10 miles west of Tillamook on Three Capes Scenic Loop.

Short Beach at Cape Meares

		Nearby Beach Access		Rating:	

Mgd by: State Parks
Parking Lot: no
  "   roadside – **many**

Drinking water   no
Tables/benches   no
Restrooms   no
Camping   no
Showers   no
Phone   no
Info Center   no
Fee   no
[Good steps down to beach]

Nearby Beach Access
Pedestrian   **yes**
Vehicle   **yes**
Boat   no

Recreation
Horse riding   no
Tidepooling   no
WhaleWatching no
Surfing   no
Bicycling   no
Hiking/trails   no
Boating   no

Rating:
★ ★ ★ ★ ☆

This is a very popular spot with the locals. There is a State SSV a short way up the road that is worth a stop.

Astoria
Seaside
→ Tillamook
Lincoln City
Newport
Florence
Reedsport
Coos Bay
Bandon
Port Orford
Gold Beach
Brookings

Pillar Rock

Cape Meares State Park

<-- Three Capes Hwy

Short Beach -->

Aerial photo courtesy of U.S. Geological Survey, 27May94   ***Width is approx. 2 miles***

On Three Capes Highway; see Cape Meares SSV.

Oceanside Beach State Recreation Site

		Nearby Beach Access		Rating:
Mgd by:	State Parks			★★★☆☆
Parking Lot:	**large**	Pedestrian	**yes**	
" roadside –	no	Vehicle	**yes**	
		Boat	no	Gets crowded
Drinking water	no			and parking
Tables/benches	**yes**	Recreation		can be hard to
Restrooms	**yes**	Horse riding	no	find at times.
Camping	no	Tidepooling	no	Three Arch
Showers	no	WhaleWatching	no	Rocks National
Phone	no	Surfing	**yes**	Wildlife
Info Center	no	Bicycling	no	Refuge.
Fee	no	Hiking/trails	no	
[Hang-gliding to the north] Boating			no	

Astoria
Seaside
→ Tillamook
Lincoln City
Newport
Florence
Reedsport
Coos Bay
Bandon
Port Orford
Gold Beach
Brookings

<-- Lost Boy Cave

<-- Agate Beach

Oceanside
Beach -->

Oceanside

Aerial photo courtesy of U.S. Geological Survey, 27May94   **Width is approx. 2 miles**

On Three Capes Scenic Loop, 11 miles west of Tillamook.

Netarts Area

Mgd by: Tillamook Co.	Nearby Beach Access	
Parking Lot: **small**	Pedestrian	**yes**
" roadside – **a few**	Vehicle	**yes**
	Boat	no
Drinking water no		
Tables/benches **yes**	**Recreation**	
Restrooms **yes**	Horse riding	no
Camping no	Tidepooling	no
Showers no	WhaleWatching	no
Phone no	Surfing	no
Info Center no	Bicycling	no
Fee no	Hiking/trails	no
[Crabbing, clamming]	Boating	**yes**

Rating:
★☆☆☆☆

Lots of varied wildlife. Use Happy Camp Road at far north end of Netarts and go to end of road. Especially beautiful on a sunny day.

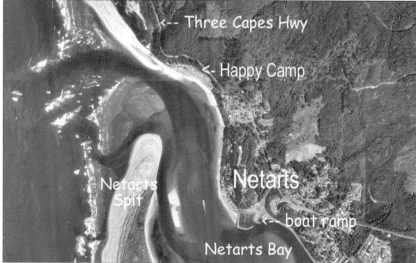

Aerial photo courtesy of U.S. Geological Survey, 27May94　　**Width is approx. 2 miles**

On Three Capes Scenic Loop, 11 miles west of Tillamook.

24

Cape Lookout State Park

		Nearby Beach Access		Rating:	
Mgd by:	State Parks	Pedestrian	**yes**	★★★★☆	Astoria
Parking Lot:	**many**	Vehicle	**yes**		Seaside
" roadside –	no	Boat	no	2,014 acres	Tillamook
					Lincoln City
Drinking water	**yes**			Many varied	Newport
Tables/benches	**yes**	Recreation		activities. 2½	
Restrooms	**yes**	Horse riding	no	mile trail to	Florence
Camping	**yes**	Tidepooling	**yes**	cape's tip. Kay-	Reedsport
Showers	**yes**	WhaleWatching	**yes**	aking.	Coos Bay
Phone	**yes**	Surfing	no	Long hikes	Bandon
Info Center	**yes**	Bicycling	**yes**	north on	Port Orford
Fee	**yes**	Hiking/trails	**yes**	Netarts Spit.	Gold Beach
[Hang-gliding: experts only] Boating			**yes**		Brookings

Cape Lookout State Park -->

Three Capes Hwy -->

Jackson Creek

Aerial photo courtesy of U.S. Geological Survey, 27May94 **Width is approx. 2 miles**

On Three Capes Scenic Loop, 12 miles west of Tillamook.

Cape Kiwanda State Natural Area

Mgd by: State Parks	Nearby Beach Access		Rating:
Parking Lot: **small**	Pedestrian	**yes**	★★★☆☆
" roadside – **yes**	Vehicle	**yes**	
	Boat	no	185 acres
Drinking water no			
Tables/benches no	**Recreation**		Mc Phillips &
Restrooms no	Horse riding	no	Tierra del Mar
Camping no	Tidepooling	**yes**	to the north
Showers no	WhaleWatching	**yes**	border this
Phone no	Surfing	**yes**	same beach.
Info Center no	Bicycling	no	Cars on the
Fee no	Hiking/trails	**yes**	beach OK.
[Hang-gliding; wave-sculpted cliffs] Boating		**yes**	

Astoria
Seaside
→ Tillamook
Lincoln City
Newport
Florence
Reedsport
Coos Bay
Bandon
Port Orford
Gold Beach
Brookings

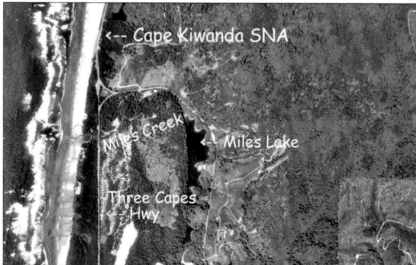

<-- Cape Kiwanda SNA

Miles Creek

Miles Lake

Three Capes Hwy

Aerial photo courtesy of U.S. Geological Survey, 27May94 **Width is approx. 2 miles**

One mile north of Pacific City. [Whalen Island County Park is nearby.]

Cape Kiwanda Launch

		Nearby Beach Access		Rating:	
Mgd by:	State Parks	Pedestrian	**yes**	★★★☆☆	Astoria
Parking Lot:	**large**	Vehicle	**yes**		Seaside
" roadside –	no	Boat	**yes**	Known for	Tillamook →
				its beach-	Lincoln City
Drinking water	no			launched	Newport
Tables/benches	**yes**	Recreation		fishing boats.	Florence
Restrooms	**yes**	Horse riding	**yes**	"The Home of	Reedsport
Camping	no	Tidepooling	**yes**	the Dory Fleet"	Coos Bay
Showers	no	WhaleWatching	**yes**	and 'the other'	Bandon
Phone	no	Surfing	**yes**	offshore Hay-	Port Orford
Info Center	no	Bicycling	no	stack Rock.	Gold Beach
Fee	no	Hiking/trails	**yes**		Brookings
[Hang gliding on cape's north side]		Boating	**yes**		

Aerial photo courtesy of U.S. Geological Survey, 27May94   ***Width is approx. 2 miles***

On Three Capes Highway at Pacific City.

Bob Straub State Park

		Nearby Beach Access		Rating:
Mgd by:	State Parks			★ ★ ★ ☆ ☆
Parking Lot:	**large**	Pedestrian	**yes**	
" roadside –	no	Vehicle	**yes**	
		Boat	**yes**	Bob Straub
Drinking water	**yes**			was a former
Tables/benches	**yes**	Recreation		governor; this
Restrooms	**yes**	Horse riding	**yes**	was originally
Camping	no	Tidepooling	no	called
Showers	no	WhaleWatching	no	Nestucca Spit.
Phone	no	Surfing	no	Still pretty
Info Center	no	Bicycling	no	much
Fee	no	Hiking/trails	no	undeveloped.
[Kayaking, clams, crabs]		Boating	**yes**	

Astoria
Seaside
→ Tillamook
Lincoln City
Newport
Florence
Reedsport
Coos Bay
Bandon
Port Orford
Gold Beach
Brookings

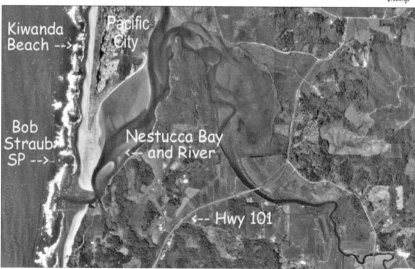

Kiwanda Beach -->
Pacific City
Bob Straub SP -->
Nestucca Bay <-- and River
<-- Hwy 101

Aerial photo courtesy of U.S. Geological Survey, 27May94   **Width is approx. 2 miles**

At Pacific City, on Nestucca River sand spit.

Neskowin Beach State Recreation Area

		Nearby Beach Access		Rating:	
Mgd by:	State Parks			★ ★ ★ ☆ ☆	Astoria
Parking Lot:	**large**	Pedestrian	**yes**		Seaside
" roadside –	no	Vehicle	**yes**		Tillamook
		Boat	no	An access	→ Lincoln City
Drinking water	no			point close to	Newport
Tables/benches	no	Recreation		the beach has	
Restrooms	**yes**	Horse riding	**yes**	some roadside	Florence
Camping	no	Tidepooling	no	parking.	Reedsport
Showers	no	WhaleWatching	no	"Welcome.	Coos Bay
Phone	no	Surfing	no	Please leave	Bandon
Info Center	no	Bicycling	**yes**	only your	Port Orford
Fee	no	Hiking/trails	no	footprints."	Gold Beach
[Proposal Rock is a landmark]		Boating	no		Brookings

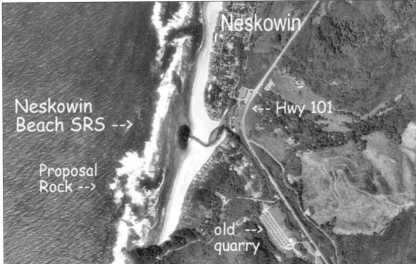

Aerial photo courtesy of U.S. Geological Survey, 27May94 **Width is approx. 2 miles**

Off US 101, 9 miles north of Lincoln City.

Cascade Head / Knight Park

Mgd by: Lincoln Co.
Parking Lot: **large**
  " roadside – **many**

Drinking water   no
Tables/benches   no
Restrooms   **yes**
Camping   no
Showers   no
Phone   no
Info Center   no
Fee   no
[Kayaking, rafting]

<u>Nearby Beach Access</u>
Pedestrian   no
Vehicle   no
Boat   **yes**

<u>Recreation</u>
Horse riding   no
Tidepooling   no
WhaleWatching   no
Surfing   no
Bicycling   **yes**
Hiking/trails   **yes**
Boating   **yes**

Rating:
★ ★ ☆ ☆ ☆

Cascade Head
Natural Area is
1,670 acres

Very popular
for all forms of
boating. Beach
is reached only
by boat.

→ Astoria
Seaside
Tillamook
Lincoln City
Newport
Florence
Reedsport
Coos Bay
Bandon
Port Orford
Gold Beach
Brookings

Cascade Head

<-- Salmon River

<-- boat ramp

Three Rocks

<-- Knight Park
with boat ramp

Aerial photo courtesy of U.S. Geological Survey, 27May94   **Width is approx. 2 miles**

At the end of Three Rocks Road, 2½ miles west off US 101, 5 miles north of Lincoln City.

Roads End State Recreation Site

		Nearby Beach Access		Rating:
Mgd by:	State Parks	Pedestrian	yes	★ ★ ★
Parking Lot:	large	Vehicle	yes	
" roadside –	a few	Boat	no	Easy access to
				a nice beach.
Drinking water	yes			Cascade Head
Tables/benches	yes	Recreation		is just to the
Restrooms	yes	Horse riding	no	north.
Camping	no	Tidepooling	no	
Showers	no	WhaleWatching	no	
Phone	no	Surfing	yes	
Info Center	no	Bicycling	no	
Fee	no	Hiking/trails	no	
[Very built-up area]		Boating	no	

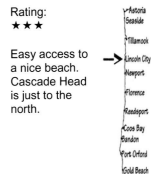

Aerial photo courtesy of U.S. Geological Survey, 27May94   ***Width is approx. 2 miles***

One mile north of Lincoln City, off US 101.

Wecoma Beach

		Nearby Beach Access		Rating:
Mgd by:	Lincoln City	Pedestrian	yes	★ ★ ★ ☆ ☆
Parking Lot:	**small**	Vehicle	yes	
" roadside –	no	Boat	no	Small, but a clean and nice place. It's away from the town crowds.
Drinking water	**yes**			
Tables/benches	**yes**	Recreation		
Restrooms	**yes**	Horse riding	no	
Camping	no	Tidepooling	no	
Showers	no	WhaleWatching	no	
Phone	no	Surfing	no	
Info Center	no	Bicycling	no	
Fee	no	Hiking/trails	no	
[Good steps to beach]		Boating	no	

⤷Astoria
Seaside
Tillamook
→ Lincoln City
Newport
Florence
Reedsport
Coos Bay
Bandon
Port Orford
Gold Beach
Brookings

Roads End

<-- Hwy 101

Wecoma Beach -->

Lake Point

Lincoln City

Devil's Lake

Aerial photo courtesy of U.S. Geological Survey, 27May94   ***Width is approx. 2 miles***

Off US 101, at the very north end of Lincoln City, at the end of NW 26th St.

D River State Recreation Site

		Nearby Beach Access		Rating:	
Mgd by:	State Parks			★ ★ ★ ☆ ☆	Astoria
Parking Lot:	**large**	Pedestrian	**yes**		Seaside
" roadside –	no	Vehicle	**yes**		Tillamook
		Boat	no	Devils Lake	Lincoln City
Drinking water	**yes**			State Park,	Newport
Tables/benches	**yes**	Recreation		east of Hwy	
Restrooms	**yes**	Horse riding	no	101, has all	Florence
Camping	no	Tidepooling	no	facilities.	Reedsport
Showers	no	WhaleWatching	**yes**		Coos Bay
Phone	no	Surfing	**yes**		Bandon
Info Center	no	Bicycling	no		Port Orford
Fee	no	Hiking/trails	no		Gold Beach
[Popular kite flying area]		Boating	no		Brookings

Aerial photo courtesy of U.S. Geological Survey, 27May94   **Width is approx. 2 miles**

On US 101, at the north end of Lincoln City .

Schooner Creek

		Nearby Beach Access		Rating:
Mgd by: Lincoln City				★★★☆☆
Parking Lot:	**large**	Pedestrian	**yes**	
" roadside –	no	Vehicle	**yes**	
		Boat	**yes**	Many large
Drinking water	**yes**			condos, hotels
Tables/benches	**yes**	Recreation		and
Restrooms	**yes**	Horse riding	no	restaurants
Camping	no	Tidepooling	no	nearby.
Showers	no	WhaleWatching	no	
Phone	no	Surfing	**yes**	
Info Center	no	Bicycling	no	
Fee	no	Hiking/trails	no	
[Well-kept area]		Boating	no	

Astoria
Seaside
Tillamook
→ Lincoln City
Newport
Florence
Reedsport
Coos Bay
Bandon
Port Orford
Gold Beach
Brookings

Aerial photo courtesy of U.S. Geological Survey, 27May94 **Width is approx. 2 miles**

At the very south end of Lincoln City, at the far west end of 51st St.

Siletz Bay Park

Mgd by: Lincoln City	Nearby Beach Access		Rating:
Parking Lot: **medium**	Pedestrian	**yes**	★ ★ ★ ☆ ☆
" roadside – no	Vehicle	**yes**	
	Boat	**yes**	Nice, but it's
Drinking water **yes**			right behind a
Tables/benches **yes**	Recreation		looming, large
Restrooms **yes**	Horse riding	no	condominiums
Camping no	Tidepooling	no	building.
Showers no	WhaleWatching	no	Best when
Phone no	Surfing	no	the tide is in.
Info Center **yes**	Bicycling	no	
Fee no	Hiking/trails	no	
[Very well-kept area]	Boating	no	

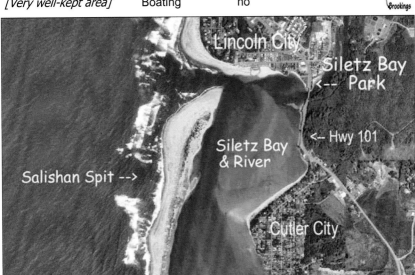

Aerial photo courtesy of U.S. Geological Survey, 27May94   **Width is approx. 2 miles**

Off US 101, at the southern-most end of Lincoln City.

Gleneden Beach State Recreation Site

		Nearby Beach Access		Rating:	
Mgd by:	State Parks	Pedestrian	**yes**	★ ★ ★ ☆ ☆	
Parking Lot:	**large**	Vehicle	**yes**		
" roadside –	no	Boat	no	Not as visited	
				as some parks,	→
Drinking water	**yes**			but it is popular	
Tables/benches	**yes**	Recreation		for surfing.	
Restrooms	**yes**	Horse riding	no		
Camping	no	Tidepooling	no		
Showers	no	WhaleWatching	no		
Phone	no	Surfing	**yes**		
Info Center	no	Bicycling	no		
Fee	no	Hiking/trails	no		
[Very residential area]		Boating	no		

Astoria
Seaside
Tillamook
Lincoln City
Newport
Florence
Reedsport
Coos Bay
Bandon
Port Orford
Gold Beach
Brookings

Gleneden
Beach

Salishan
Golf Course

Gleneden
Beach SRS -->

Siletz Bay
State Airport

<-- Hwy 101

Aerial photo courtesy of U.S. Geological Survey, 27May94   ***Width is approx. 2 miles***

Seven miles south of Lincoln City, off US 101.

Fishing Rock

		Nearby Beach Access		Rating:	
Mgd by:	State Parks			★ ★ ☆ ☆ ☆	Astoria
Parking Lot:	**small**	Pedestrian	**yes**		Seaside
" roadside –	**a few**	Vehicle	**yes**		Tillamook
		Boat	no	Good trail to	Lincoln City
Drinking water	no			the bluff is	Newport
Tables/benches	no	Recreation		about 200	
Restrooms	no	Horse riding	no	yards long.	Florence
Camping	no	Tidepooling	no	A pleasant	Reedsport
Showers	no	WhaleWatching	no	walk.	Coos Bay
Phone	no	Surfing	no		Bandon
Info Center	no	Bicycling	no		Port Orford
Fee	no	Hiking/trails	no		Gold Beach
[Broad, grassy picnic area]		Boating	no		Brookings

Aerial photo courtesy of U.S. Geological Survey, 27May94   **Width is approx. 2 miles**

Off US 101, at the south end of Lincoln Beach.

Fogarty Creek State Recreation Area

Mgd by: State Parks	<u>Nearby Beach Access</u>		Rating:	Astoria
Parking Lot: **large**	Pedestrian	**yes**	★ ★ ★ ☆ ☆	Seaside
" roadside – no	Vehicle	**yes**		Tillamook
	Boat	no	142 acres	Lincoln City
Drinking water **yes**				→ Newport
Tables/benches **yes**	<u>Recreation</u>		A spouting	
Restrooms **yes**	Horse riding	no	horn is in the	Florence
Camping no	Tidepooling	**yes**	southern rocks.	Reedsport
Showers no	WhaleWatching	no	A very popular	Coos Bay
Phone no	Surfing	no	park.	Bandon
Info Center no	Bicycling	no		Port Orford
Fee **yes**	Hiking/trails	**yes**		Gold Beach
[Interesting Offshore rocks]	Boating	no		Brookings

Aerial photo courtesy of U.S. Geological Survey, 27May94   **Width is approx. 2 miles**

Off US 101, 2 miles north of Depoe Bay.

Devil's Punch Bowl State Natural Area, at Otter Crest

Mgd by: State Parks		Nearby Beach Access		Rating:	
Parking Lot:	**large**	Pedestrian	**yes**	★★★☆☆	
" roadside –	no	Vehicle	**yes**		
		Boat	no	4 acres	
Drinking water	**yes**				
Tables/benches	**yes**	Recreation		Cape	
Restrooms	**yes**	Horse riding	no	Foulweather is	
Camping	no	Tidepooling	**yes**	just north.	
Showers	no	WhaleWatching	**yes**	Especially	
Phone	no	Surfing	**yes**	popular with	
Info Center	**yes**	Bicycling	no	surfers. Good,	
Fee	no	Hiking/trails	**yes**	but long steps	
[Collapsed sea cave]		Boating	no		

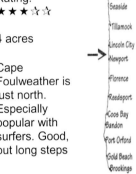

Astoria
Seaside
Tillamook
Lincoln City
→ Newport
Florence
Reedsport
Coos Bay
Bandon
Port Orford
Gold Beach
Brookings

Aerial photo courtesy of U.S. Geological Survey, 27May94 **Width is approx. 2 miles**

Off US 101, 8 miles north of Newport.

Beverly Beach State Park

Mgd by: State Parks
Parking Lot: **large**
" roadside – no

Drinking water **yes**
Tables/benches **yes**
Restrooms **yes**
Camping **yes**
Showers **yes**
Phone **yes**
Info Center **yes**
Fee (day use no) **yes**
[Popular camping spot]

<u>Nearby Beach Access</u>
Pedestrian **yes**
Vehicle **yes**
Boat no

<u>Recreation</u>
Horse riding no
Tidepooling no
WhaleWatching **yes**
Surfing **yes**
Bicycling no
Hiking/trails **yes**
Boating no

Rating:
★ ★ ★ ☆ ☆

130 acres

Nature trail
along Spencer
Creek. Good
kite flying and
excellent
surfing.

Astoria
Seaside
Tillamook
Lincoln City
→ Newport
Florence
Reedsport
Coos Bay
Bandon
Port Orford
Gold Beach
Brookings

Aerial photo courtesy of U.S. Geological Survey, 27May94   ***Width is approx. 2 miles***

Off US 101, 7 miles north of Newport.

Wade Creek

Mgd by:	ODOT	Nearby Beach Access		Rating:
Parking Lot:	no	Pedestrian	**yes**	★ ★ ☆ ☆ ☆
" roadside –	**yes**	Vehicle	**yes**	
		Boat	no	Entrance is
Drinking water	no			through the
Tables/benches	no	Recreation		trees at the
Restrooms	no	Horse riding	no	south end of
Camping	no	Tidepooling	no	the parking lot.
Showers	no	WhaleWatching	no	Leave your car
Phone	no	Surfing	no	on top and
Info Center	no	Bicycling	no	walk down.
Fee	no	Hiking/trails	no	
		Boating	no	

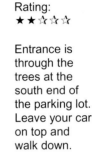

Astoria
Seaside
Tillamook
Lincoln City
➡ Newport
Florence
Reedsport
Coos Bay
Bandon
Port Orford
Gold Beach
Brookings

Wade Creek -->
<-- Hwy 101
Coal Creek

Aerial photo courtesy of U.S. Geological Survey, 27May94   ***Width is approx. 2 miles***

Off US 101, 6 miles north of Newport.

Moolack Beach

Mgd by:	OPRD	Nearby Beach Access		Rating:
Parking Lot: **medium**		Pedestrian	**yes**	★★★☆☆
" roadside –	no	Vehicle	**yes**	
		Boat	no	Good
Drinking water	no			beachcombing
Tables/benches	no	Recreation		and agate
Restrooms	no	Horse riding	no	hunting after a
Camping	no	Tidepooling	no	storm.
Showers	no	WhaleWatching	**yes**	
Phone	no	Surfing	**yes**	
Info Center	no	Bicycling	no	
Fee	no	Hiking/trails	no	
[Yaquina Head Lighthouse] Boating			no	

Astoria
Seaside
Tillamook
Lincoln City
→ Newport
Florence
Reedsport
Coos Bay
Bandon
Port Orford
Gold Beach
Brookings

Aerial photo courtesy of U.S. Geological Survey, 27May94   ***Width is approx. 2 miles***

Off US 101, 3½ miles north of Newport.

Yaquina Head Outstanding Natural Area

Mgd by:	BLM	**Nearby Beach Access**		Rating:		Astoria
Parking Lot:	**large**	Pedestrian	**yes**	★★★★☆		Seaside
" roadside –	no	Vehicle	no			Tillamook
		Boat	no	100 acres		Lincoln City
Drinking water	no				→	Newport
Tables/benches	no	**Recreation**		Tallest light-		Florence
Restrooms	**yes**	Horse riding	no	house on the		Reedsport
Camping	no	Tidepooling	**yes**	coast.		Coos Bay
Showers	no	WhaleWatching	**yes**	Wheelchair		Bandon
Phone	no	Surfing	**yes**	accessible tide		Port Orford
Info Center	**yes**	Bicycling	no	pools.		Gold Beach
Fee	**yes**	Hiking/trails	**yes**	Former quarry.		Brookings
[Yaquina Head Lighthouse]		Boating	no			

Aerial photo courtesy of U.S. Geological Survey, 27May94   **Width is approx. 2 miles**

Off US 101, 2 miles north of Newport.

Agate Beach State Recreation Site

		Nearby Beach Access		Rating:	
Mgd by:	State Parks			★ ★ ★ ☆ ☆	Astoria
Parking Lot: **medium**		Pedestrian	**yes**		Seaside
" roadside –	no	Vehicle	**yes**		Tillamook
		Boat	no	Turn off Hwy	Lincoln City
Drinking water	**yes**			101 at north	→ Newport
Tables/benches	**yes**	Recreation		end of town,	
Restrooms	**yes**	Horse riding	no	onto NW	Florence
Camping	no	Tidepooling	no	Oceanview	Reedsport
Showers	no	WhaleWatching	no	Drive. Two	Coos Bay
Phone	no	Surfing	**yes**	parking areas.	Bandon
Info Center	no	Bicycling	no		Port Orford
Fee	no	Hiking/trails	no		Gold Beach
[Yaquina Head Lighthouse]		Boating	no		Brookings

Aerial photo courtesy of U.S. Geological Survey, 27May94   ***Width is approx. 2 miles***

Off US 101, one mile north of Newport.

Nye Beach / Jump Off Joe

		Nearby Beach Access		Rating:	
Mgd by:	Newport			★ ★ ★ ☆ ☆	
Parking Lot: **medium**		Pedestrian	**yes**		
" roadside –	no	Vehicle	**yes**		
		Boat	no	Right in town,	
Drinking water	**yes**			but included	
Tables/benches	**yes**	Recreation		because it is	
Restrooms	**yes**	Horse riding	no	very well-	
Camping	no	Tidepooling	no	known and the	
Showers	no	WhaleWatching	no	beach is	
Phone	no	Surfing	no	spacious.	
Info Center	no	Bicycling	no	Next to the Art	
Fee	no	Hiking/trails	no	Center.	
[Foot wash faucet]		Boating	no		

Astoria
Seaside
Tillamook
Lincoln City
→ Newport
Florence
Reedsport
Coos Bay
Bandon
Port Orford
Gold Beach
Brookings

Aerial photo courtesy of U.S. Geological Survey, 27May94 **Width is approx. 2 miles**

From US 101 take NW 6th St to NW Coast St, left turn to NW Beach Drive.

Yaquina Bay State Recreation Site

		Nearby Beach Access		Rating:	
Mgd by:	State Parks			★★★☆☆	Astoria
Parking Lot:	**several**	Pedestrian	**yes**		Seaside
" roadside –	no	Vehicle	**yes**		Tillamook
		Boat	no	32 acres	Lincoln City
Drinking water	**yes**				→ Newport
Tables/benches	**yes**	Recreation		Lighthouse is	Florence
Restrooms	**yes**	Horse riding	no	open as a	Reedsport
Camping	no	Tidepooling	no	museum daily.	
Showers	no	WhaleWatching	**yes**	Two-hour	Coos Bay
Phone	no	Surfing	**yes**	naturalist	Bandon
Info Center	**yes**	Bicycling	no	cruises:	Port Orford
Fee	no	Hiking/trails	**yes**	whales, seals,	Gold Beach
[Yaquina Bay Lighthouse]	Boating	no	sea lions, birds.	Brookings

Aerial photo courtesy of U.S. Geological Survey, 27May94   ***Width is approx. 2 miles***

North end of the Yaquina Bay Bridge, Newport.

South Beach State Park

			Nearby Beach Access		Rating:	

Mgd by: State Parks
Parking Lot: **many**
"   roadside –   no

Drinking water   **yes**
Tables/benches   **yes**
Restrooms   **yes**
Camping   **yes**
Showers   **yes**
Phone   **yes**
Info Center   **yes**
Fee   **yes**
[Kayaking, clamming]

Nearby Beach Access
Pedestrian   **yes**
Vehicle   **yes**
Boat   no

Recreation
Horse riding   no
Tidepooling   no
WhaleWatching   no
Surfing   **yes**
Bicycling   **yes**
Hiking/trails   **yes**
Boating   **yes**

Rating:
★ ★ ★ ★ ☆

434 acres

Playground,
volley
& basketball
areas. Easy
hike along the
beach north to
the jetty.

Astoria
Seaside
Tillamook
Lincoln City
→ Newport
Florence
Reedsport
Coos Bay
Bandon
Port Orford
Gold Beach
Brookings

Aerial photo courtesy of U.S. Geological Survey, 27May94   **Width is approx. 2 miles**

Off US 101, 2 miles south of Newport.

Lost Creek State Recreation Site

Mgd by: State Parks
Parking Lot: **medium**
" roadside – no

Drinking water **yes**
Tables/benches **yes**
Restrooms **yes**
Camping no
Showers no
Phone no
Info Center no
Fee no

Nearby Beach Access
Pedestrian **yes**
Vehicle **yes**
Boat no

Recreation
Horse riding no
Tidepooling no
WhaleWatching no
Surfing no
Bicycling no
Hiking/trails no
Boating no

Rating:
★ ★ ☆ ☆ ☆

34 acres

Access is
through the
SRS and also
there's an
emergency
beach access
road at the
south end.

Astoria
Seaside
Tillamook
Lincoln City
→ Newport
Florence
Reedsport
Coos Bay
Bandon
Port Orford
Gold Beach
Brookings

Aerial photo courtesy of U.S. Geological Survey, 27May94   ***Width is approx. 2 miles***

Off US 101, 6 miles south of Newport.

Ona Beach State Park

Mgd by: State Parks		<u>Nearby Beach Access</u>		Rating:	Astoria
Parking Lot:	**large**	Pedestrian	**yes**	★ ★ ★ ★ ☆	Seaside
" roadside –	no	Vehicle	**yes**		Tillamook
		Boat	no	237 acres	Lincoln City
Drinking water	**yes**				Newport
Tables/benches	**yes**	<u>Recreation</u>		Great spot for	
Restrooms	**yes**	Horse riding	no	a picnic lunch	Florence
Camping	no	Tidepooling	no	and then a	Reedsport
Showers	no	WhaleWatching	no	pleasant stroll	Coos Bay
Phone	no	Surfing	**yes**	through the	Bandon
Info Center	no	Bicycling	no	park to the	Port Orford
Fee	no	Hiking/trails	**yes**	beach.	Gold Beach
[Kayaking, canoeing]		Boating	**yes**		Brookings

Aerial photo courtesy of U.S. Geological Survey, 27May94   **Width is approx. 2 miles**

Off US 101, 7½ miles south of Newport.

Hwy 101 at Curtis Street

Mgd by:	ODOT	<u>Nearby Beach Access</u>		Rating:		✈Astoria
Parking Lot:	**small**	Pedestrian	**yes**	★ ★ ☆ ☆ ☆		Seaside
" roadside –	no	Vehicle	**yes**			Tillamook
		Boat	no	This is an		Lincoln City
Drinking water	no			emergency		Newport
Tables/benches	no	<u>Recreation</u>		beach access	→	
Restrooms	no	Horse riding	no	road; no public		Florence
Camping	no	Tidepooling	no	vehicle use.		Reedsport
Showers	no	WhaleWatching	no	Near MP 150,		Coos Bay
Phone	no	Surfing	no	a little south of		Bandon
Info Center	no	Bicycling	no	Ona SP.		Port Orford
Fee	no	Hiking/trails	no			Gold Beach
[Just north of Seal Rock]		Boating	no			Brookings

<-- Hwy 101

Curtis Street →

Seal Rock

Aerial photo courtesy of U.S. Geological Survey, 27May94   ***Width is approx. 2 miles***

Off US 101, 9 miles south of Newport.

Seal Rock State Recreation Site

		Nearby Beach Access		Rating:
Mgd by:	State Parks			★ ★ ★ ☆ ☆
Parking Lot:	**medium**	Pedestrian	**yes**	
" roadside –	no	Vehicle	**yes**	Harbor seals,
		Boat	no	sea lions;
Drinking water	**yes**			great place
Tables/benches	**yes**	Recreation		for
Restrooms	**yes**	Horse riding	no	photos.
Camping	no	Tidepooling	**yes**	
Showers	no	WhaleWatching	**yes**	
Phone	no	Surfing	no	
Info Center	**yes**	Bicycling	no	
Fee	no	Hiking/trails	**yes**	
[Large offshore rocks]		Boating	no	

Astoria
Seaside
Tillamook
Lincoln City
Newport →
Florence
Reedsport
Coos Bay
Bandon
Port Orford
Gold Beach
Brookings

Seal Rock SRS -->
<-- Hwy 101
Seal Rock

Aerial photo courtesy of U.S. Geological Survey, 27May94   **Width is approx. 2 miles**

Off US 101, 9½ miles south of Newport.

Collins Creek

Mgd by: State Parks
Parking Lot: no
"   roadside – **a few**

Drinking water   no
Tables/benches   no
Restrooms   no
Camping   no
Showers   no
Phone   no
Info Center   no
Fee   no

<u>Nearby Beach Access</u>
Pedestrian   **yes**
Vehicle   **yes**
Boat   no

<u>Recreation</u>
Horse riding   no
Tidepooling   no
WhaleWatching no
Surfing   no
Bicycling   no
Hiking/trails   no
Boating   no

Rating:
★ ★ ☆ ☆ ☆

Beach access
is via a gravel
road in the
bushes at the
south end of
parking area.

→

Astoria
Seaside
Tillamook
Lincoln City
Newport
Florence
Reedsport
Coos Bay
Bandon
Port Orford
Gold Beach
Brookings

Aerial photo courtesy of U.S. Geological Survey, 27May94   **Width is approx. 2 miles**

Off US 101, 10½ miles south of Newport.

Driftwood Beach State Recreation Site

		Nearby Beach Access		Rating:
Mgd by:	State Parks			★★★☆☆
Parking Lot:	**medium**	Pedestrian	**yes**	
" roadside –	no	Vehicle	**yes**	This is a good
		Boat	no	but somewhat
Drinking water	**yes**			overlooked
Tables/benches	**yes**	Recreation		place.
Restrooms	**yes**	Horse riding	no	
Camping	no	Tidepooling	no	
Showers	no	WhaleWatching	no	
Phone	no	Surfing	no	
Info Center	no	Bicycling	no	
Fee	no	Hiking/trails	no	
		Boating	no	

Astoria
Seaside
Tillamook
Lincoln City
Newport
→
Florence
Reedsport
Coos Bay
Bandon
Port Orford
Gold Beach
Brookings

Fox Creek

<-- Hwy 101

Driftwood Beach SRS -->

Siuslaw National Forest

Aerial photo courtesy of U.S. Geological Survey, 27May94   ***Width is approx. 2 miles***

Off US 101, 3 miles north of Waldport.

William P. Keady Wayside

Mgd by: State Parks
Parking Lot: **small**
  "   roadside – **a few**

Drinking water   no
Tables/benches   **yes**
Restrooms   **yes**
Camping   no
Showers   no
Phone   no
Info Center   no
Fee   no
[Clams, crabbing]

Nearby Beach Access
Pedestrian   **yes**
Vehicle   **yes**
Boat   no

Recreation
Horse riding   no
Tidepooling   no
WhaleWatching   no
Surfing   no
Bicycling   no
Hiking/trails   no
Boating   no

Rating:
★ ★ ☆ ☆ ☆

Small, but nice.
Coastal
Bridges
Interpretive
Center at south
end of the
bridge.

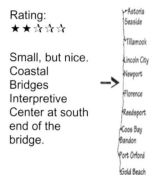

Astoria
Seaside
Tillamook
Lincoln City
Newport
Florence
Reedsport
Coos Bay
Bandon
Port Orford
Gold Beach
Brookings

Aerial photo courtesy of U.S. Geological Survey, 27May94   ***Width is approx. 2 miles***

At the very south end of Waldport.

54

Governor Patterson Memorial State Recreation Site

		Nearby Beach Access		Rating:	
Mgd by:	State Parks			★ ★ ★ ☆ ☆	Astoria
Parking Lot:	**large**	Pedestrian	**yes**		Seaside
" roadside –	no	Vehicle	**yes**		Tillamook
		Boat	no	10 acres	Lincoln City
Drinking water	no				Newport
Tables/benches	**yes**	Recreation		You can walk	→
Restrooms	**yes**	Horse riding	no	south for 7	Florence
Camping	no	Tidepooling	no	miles on the	Reedsport
Showers	no	WhaleWatching	no	beach, to a	Coos Bay
Phone	no	Surfing	no	small	Bandon
Info Center	no	Bicycling	no	headland.	Port Orford
Fee	no	Hiking/trails	**yes**		Gold Beach
[Alsea Bay: crabbing, clams]		Boating	no		Brookings

Yaquina John Point - →

golf course

Patterson SP ← – – –

← Hwy 101

Lint Creek - →

Aerial photo courtesy of U.S. Geological Survey, 27May94   **Width is approx. 2 miles**

Off US 101, one mile south of Waldport.

Highway 101 at Whitecap Drive

		Nearby Beach Access		Rating:	
Mgd by:	ODOT			★ ★ ☆ ☆ ☆	
Parking Lot:	no	Pedestrian	**yes**		
"roadside – **several**		Vehicle	**yes**		
		Boat	no	A bit rough but	
Drinking water	no			short trail down	
Tables/benches	no	Recreation		from a low	
Restrooms	no	Horse riding	no	bluff. Miles of	
Camping	no	Tidepooling	no	nice, sandy	
Showers	no	WhaleWatching	no	beach.	
Phone	no	Surfing	no		
Info Center	no	Bicycling	no		
Fee	no	Hiking/trails	no		
		Boating	no		

Aerial photo courtesy of U.S. Geological Survey, 27May94　　**Width is approx. 2 miles**

Off Hwy 101, 1½ miles south of Waldport; 6½ miles north of Yachats.

Highway 101 at Wakonda Beach Road (Milepost 159)

Mgd by:	ODOT	Nearby Beach Access		Rating:
Parking Lot:	no	Pedestrian	yes	★ ★ ☆ ☆ ☆
" roadside –	a few	Vehicle	yes	
		Boat	no	Above road is
Drinking water	no			for emergency
Tables/benches	no	Recreation		vehicles only.
Restrooms	no	Horse riding	no	It's a narrow
Camping	no	Tidepooling	no	access to lots
Showers	no	WhaleWatching	no	of good beach.
Phone	no	Surfing	no	
Info Center	no	Bicycling	no	
Fee	no	Hiking/trails	no	
		Boating	no	

Astoria
Seaside
Tillamook
Lincoln City
Newport
→ Florence
Reedsport
Coos Bay
Bandon
Port Orford
Gold Beach
Brookings

Milepost 159 -->
<-- Hwy 101
Waconda Beach -->
<-- landing strip

Aerial photo courtesy of U.S. Geological Survey, 27May94   **Width is approx. 2 miles**

Off Hwy 101, 5½ miles north of Yachats.

Beachside State Recreation Site

Mgd by:	State Parks	Nearby Beach Access		Rating:
Parking Lot:	**large**	Pedestrian	**yes**	★ ★ ★ ☆ ☆
" roadside –	no	Vehicle	**yes**	
		Boat	no	17 acres
Drinking water	**yes**			
Tables/benches	**yes**	Recreation		Campsites
Restrooms	**yes**	Horse riding	no	practically right
Camping	**yes**	Tidepooling	no	on the beach,
Showers	**yes**	WhaleWatching	no	and the access
Phone	**yes**	Surfing	no	is very easy.
Info Center	**yes**	Bicycling	no	
Fee (day use no) **yes**		Hiking/trails	**yes**	
[Adjacent to US 101]		Boating	no	

Astoria
Seaside

Tillamook

Lincoln City

Newport

→ Florence

Reedsport

Coos Bay
Bandon

Port Orford

Gold Beach
Brookings

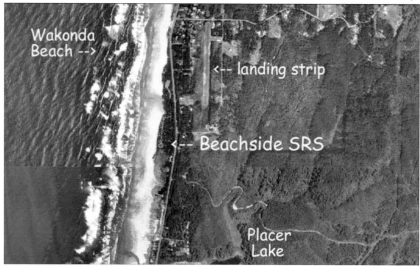

Aerial photo courtesy of U.S. Geological Survey, 27May94 **Width is approx. 2 miles**

Off US 101, 3 miles south of Waldport.

Tillicum Beach Campground

		Nearby Beach Access		Rating:	
Mgd by:	USFS	Pedestrian	**yes**	★ ★ ★ ☆ ☆	
Parking Lot: **medium**		Vehicle	**yes**		
" roadside –	no	Boat	no	On a low bluff	

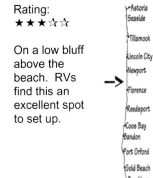

Mgd by: USFS
Parking Lot: **medium**
   "   roadside –   no

Drinking water   **yes**
Tables/benches   **yes**
Restrooms   **yes**
Camping   **yes**
Showers   no
Phone   no
Info Center   no
Fee   **yes**

Nearby Beach Access
   Pedestrian   **yes**
   Vehicle   **yes**
   Boat   no

Recreation
   Horse riding   no
   Tidepooling   no
   WhaleWatching   no
   Surfing   no
   Bicycling   no
   Hiking/trails   no
   Boating   no

Rating:
★ ★ ★ ☆ ☆

On a low bluff
above the
beach. RVs
find this an
excellent spot
to set up.

→

Astoria
Seaside
Tillamook
Lincoln City
Newport
Florence
Reedsport
Coos Bay
Bandon
Port Orford
Gold Beach
Brookings

Aerial photo courtesy of U.S. Geological Survey, 27May94   ***Width is approx. 2 miles***

Off US 101, 4 miles south of Waldport.

Vingie Lane

Mgd by:	OPRD	Nearby Beach Access		Rating:
Parking Lot:	no	Pedestrian	**yes**	★ ★ ☆ ☆ ☆
" roadside –	**yes**	Vehicle	**yes**	
		Boat	no	Good, 100
Drinking water	no			yards trail to
Tables/benches	no	Recreation		the beach.
Restrooms	no	Horse riding	no	The Lane is a
Camping	no	Tidepooling	no	street on the
Showers	no	WhaleWatching	no	east side of
Phone	no	Surfing	no	Hwy 101.
Info Center	no	Bicycling	no	
Fee	no	Hiking/trails	no	
		Boating	no	

Astoria
Seaside
Tillamook
Lincoln City
Newport
Florence
Reedsport
Coos Bay
Bandon
Port Orford
Gold Beach
Brookings

Aerial photo courtesy of U.S. Geological Survey, 27May94   **Width is approx. 2 miles**

Off US 101, 2 miles north of Yachats town center.

Smelt Sands State Recreation Site

		Nearby Beach Access		Rating:	

Mgd by: State Parks

Parking Lot: **medium**

"   roadside –   no

Astoria
Seaside
Tillamook
Lincoln City
Newport
Florence
Reedsport
Coos Bay
Bandon
Port Orford
Gold Beach
Brookings

<u>Nearby Beach Access</u>

Pedestrian	**yes**
Vehicle	**yes**
Boat	no

Drinking water	no
Tables/benches	**yes**
Restrooms	**yes**
Camping	no
Showers	no
Phone	no
Info Center	no
Fee	no
[Annual Smelt Run]	

<u>Recreation</u>

Horse riding	no
Tidepooling	**yes**
WhaleWatching	no
Surfing	no
Bicycling	no
Hiking/trails	**yes**
Boating	no

Rating:

★ ★ ★ ☆ ☆

This is at the south end of the ¾ mile Yachts 804 Trail. It's a popular walk.

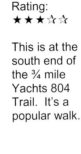

< -- Hwy 101

Starr Creek

< - - Smelt Sands SRS

Yachats

Aerial photo courtesy of U.S. Geological Survey, 27May94   **Width is approx. 2 miles**

Off US 101, 1 mile north of the Yachats River.

Yachats State Recreation Area

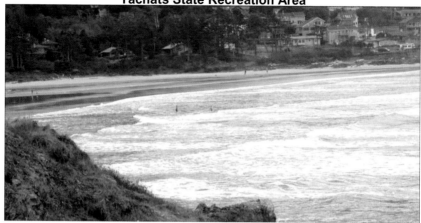

Mgd by: State Parks	Nearby Beach Access		Rating:	Astoria
Parking Lot: **medium**	Pedestrian	**yes**	★ ★ ★ ☆ ☆	Seaside
" roadside – no	Vehicle	**yes**		Tillamook
	Boat	no	94 acres	Lincoln City
Drinking water **yes**				Newport
Tables/benches **yes**	Recreation		One main	Florence
Restrooms **yes**	Horse riding	no	beach, above,	
Camping no	Tidepooling	**yes**	and several	Reedsport
Showers no	WhaleWatching	**yes**	small beaches	Coos Bay
Phone no	Surfing	no	amongst the	Bandon
Info Center no	Bicycling	no	rocks.	Port Orford
Fee no	Hiking/trails	no		Gold Beach
	Boating	no		Brookings

→

Aerial photo courtesy of U.S. Geological Survey, 27May94   **Width is approx. 2 miles**

At the mouth of the Yachats River, north side.

Yachats Ocean Road State Natural Site

Mgd by: State Parks	Nearby Beach Access		Rating:
Parking Lot: **small**	Pedestrian	**yes**	★ ★ ★ ☆ ☆
" roadside – **a few**	Vehicle	**yes**	
	Boat	no	Broad sandy
Drinking water no			beaches; also
Tables/benches **yes**	Recreation		some very
Restrooms **yes**	Horse riding	no	rocky areas.
Camping no	Tidepooling	**yes**	It's Yachats,
Showers no	WhaleWatching	**yes**	and so it is a
Phone no	Surfing	no	very popular
Info Center no	Bicycling	no	place.
Fee no	Hiking/trails	no	
[Very residential area]	Boating	no	

Astoria
Seaside
Tillamook
Lincoln City
Newport
→ Florence
Reedsport
Coos Bay
Bandon
Port Orford
Gold Beach
Brookings

Aerial photo courtesy of U.S. Geological Survey, 27May94   **Width is approx. 2 miles**

At the mouth of the Yachats River, south side.

Devil's Churn - Cape Perpetua Scenic Area

Mgd by:	USFS	Nearby Beach Access		Rating:
Parking Lot:	**medium**	Pedestrian	**yes**	★ ★ ☆ ☆ ☆
" roadside –	no	Vehicle	**yes**	
		Boat	no	A new tourist
Drinking water	**yes**			snack/espresso
Tables/benches	**yes**	Recreation		facility was built
Restrooms	**yes**	Horse riding	no	here in 2004.
Camping	no	Tidepooling	**yes**	
Showers	no	WhaleWatching	**yes**	Indoor whale
Phone	**yes**	Surfing	no	watching at the
Info Center	**yes**	Bicycling	no	main visitor
Fee	**yes**	Hiking/trails	**yes**	center.
[Also see Cook's Chasm]		Boating	no	

Astoria
Seaside
Tillamook
Lincoln City
Newport
→ Florence
Reedsport
Coos Bay
Bandon
Port Orford
Gold Beach
Brookings

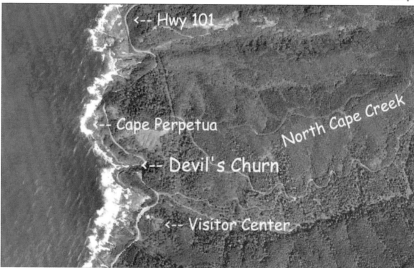

Aerial photo courtesy of U.S. Geological Survey, 27May94   **Width is approx. 2 miles**

Off US 101, 2 miles south of the Yachats River.

Cape Cove Marine Gardens

Mgd by:	USFS
Parking Lot:	**small**
" roadside –	no
Drinking water	no
Tables/benches	no
Restrooms	no
Camping	no
Showers	no
Phone	no
Info Center	no
Fee	**yes**

Nearby Beach Access

Pedestrian	**yes**
Vehicle	**yes**
Boat	no

Recreation

Horse riding	no
Tidepooling	**yes**
WhaleWatching	**yes**
Surfing	no
Bicycling	no
Hiking/trails	**yes**
Boating	no

Rating:
★ ★ ★ ☆ ☆

A place worth the short hike down, but you probably won't stay a long time. It's very self-contained.

Astoria
Seaside
Tillamook
Lincoln City
Newport
→ Florence
Reedsport
Coos Bay
Bandon
Port Orford
Gold Beach
Brookings

Captain Cook Point -->
<-- Cape Cove
<-- Cook's Chasm
Gwynn Creek
<-- Hwy 101

Aerial photo courtesy of U.S. Geological Survey, 27May94   **Width is approx. 2 miles**

Off US 101, 2½ miles south of the Yachats River.

Cook's Chasm - Cape Perpetua Scenic Area

Mgd by:	USFS	Nearby Beach Access		Rating:
Parking Lot:	**small**	Pedestrian	**yes**	★ ★ ★ ☆ ☆
" roadside –	no	Vehicle	**yes**	
		Boat	no	2,700 acres
Drinking water	no			
Tables/benches	**yes**	Recreation		Capt. Cook
Restrooms	no	Horse riding	no	trail (0.6 mi)
Camping	no	Tidepooling	**yes**	starts at the
Showers	no	WhaleWatching	**yes**	visitor center.
Phone	no	Surfing	no	Newly redone
Info Center	**yes**	Bicycling	**yes**	parking and
Fee	no	Hiking/trails	**yes**	tourist facilities.
[Remarks are for entire Area]		Boating	no	

Astoria
Seaside
Tillamook
Lincoln City
Newport
→ Florence
Reedsport
Coos Bay
Bandon
Port Orford
Gold Beach
Brookings

Aerial photo courtesy of U.S. Geological Survey, 27May94 **Width is approx. 2 miles**

Off US 101, 2¾ miles south of the Yachats River.

Cummins Creek - Neptune State Scenic Viewpoint

Mgd by: State Parks	Nearby Beach Access		Rating:
Parking Lot: **medium**	Pedestrian	**yes**	★ ★ ☆ ☆ ☆
" roadside – no	Vehicle	**yes**	
	Boat	no	Cummins
Drinking water **yes**			Creek Trail is
Tables/benches **yes**	Recreation		open to
Restrooms **yes**	Horse riding	no	mountain
Camping no	Tidepooling	**yes**	bikes.
Showers no	WhaleWatching	no	
Phone no	Surfing	no	
Info Center no	Bicycling	**yes**	
Fee no	Hiking/trails	**yes**	
	Boating	no	

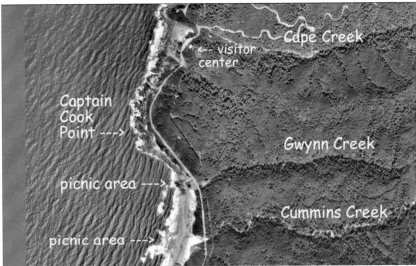

Aerial photo courtesy of U.S. Geological Survey, 27May94 **Width is approx. 2 miles**

Off US 101, 3½ miles south of the Yachats River.

Strawberry Hill - Neptune State Scenic Viewpoint

Mgd by:	State Parks	Nearby Beach Access		Rating:
Parking Lot:	**small**	Pedestrian	**yes**	★ ★ ★ ☆ ☆
" roadside –	no	Vehicle	**yes**	
		Boat	no	Neptune SP
Drinking water	no			has 302 acres.
Tables/benches	**yes**	Recreation		A protected
Restrooms	**yes**	Horse riding	no	area; see sign
Camping	no	Tidepooling	**yes**	re: collecting.
Showers	no	WhaleWatching	**yes**	Beaches good
Phone	no	Surfing	no	both north &
Info Center	no	Bicycling	no	south.
Fee	no	Hiking/trails	no	
		Boating	no	

Astoria
Seaside
Tillamook
Lincoln City
Newport
→ Florence
Reedsport
Coos Bay
Bandon
Port Orford
Gold Beach
Brookings

picnic area →

Little Cummins Creek

<-- Hwy 101

Strawberry Hill
<-- picnic area

Neptune
State
Park

Aerial photo courtesy of U.S. Geological Survey, 27May94   **Width is approx. 2 miles**

Off US 101, 4½ miles south of Yachats.

Bob Creek - Neptune State Scenic Viewpoint

		Nearby Beach Access		Rating: ★ ★ ★	
Mgd by:	State Parks	Pedestrian	**yes**		Astoria
Parking Lot:	**small**	Vehicle	**yes**		Seaside
" roadside –	no	Boat	no	Long, broad	Tillamook
				expanses of	Lincoln City
Drinking water	no			combers. A	Newport
Tables/benches	**yes**	Recreation		gravel beach;	Florence
Restrooms	**yes**	Horse riding	no	doesn't get a	Reedsport
Camping	no	Tidepooling	**yes**	lot of use.	Coos Bay
Showers	no	WhaleWatching	no		Bandon
Phone	no	Surfing	no		Port Orford
Info Center	no	Bicycling	no		Gold Beach
Fee	no	Hiking/trails	**yes**		Brookings
		Boating	no		

Neptune State Park

<-- Stawberry Hill

<-- Hwy 101   Bob Creek

<-- Gwynn Knoll

Beach & parking -->

<-- Bray Point

Aerial photo courtesy of U.S. Geological Survey, 27May94   **Width is approx. 2 miles**

Off US 101, 5½ miles south of the Yachats River.

Stonefield Beach State Recreation Site

Mgd by: State Parks		
Parking Lot: **medium**		
" roadside –	no	
Drinking water	no	
Tables/benches	no	
Restrooms	no	
Camping	no	
Showers	no	
Phone	no	
Info Center	no	
Fee	no	

Nearby Beach Access

Pedestrian	**yes**
Vehicle	**yes**
Boat	no

Recreation

Horse riding	no
Tidepooling	no
WhaleWatching	no
Surfing	no
Bicycling	no
Hiking/trails	no
Boating	no

Rating:
★ ★ ☆ ☆ ☆

The name of this beach is appropriate, but it's still a pretty nice place.

Astoria
Seaside
Tillamook
Lincoln City
Newport
Florence
Reedsport
Coos Bay
Bandon
Port Orford
Gold Beach
Brookings

Aerial photo courtesy of U.S. Geological Survey, 27May94   **Width is approx. 2 miles**

Off US 101, 5½ miles south of the Yachats River.

Ocean Beach

Mgd by:	USFS	Nearby Beach Access		Rating:
Parking Lot:	**small**	Pedestrian	**yes**	★ ★ ★ ☆ ☆
" roadside –	**a few**	Vehicle	**yes**	
		Boat	no	Great place for
Drinking water	no			a picnic, or to
Tables/benches	**yes**	Recreation		spend the day
Restrooms	**yes**	Horse riding	no	on the beach.
Camping	no	Tidepooling	no	Off by itself,
Showers	no	WhaleWatching	no	but not at all
Phone	no	Surfing	no	isolated.
Info Center	no	Bicycling	no	
Fee	no	Hiking/trails	no	
		Boating	no	

Aerial photo courtesy of U.S. Geological Survey, 27May94   **Width is approx. 2 miles**

Off US 101, 8½ miles south of the Yachats River.

Muriel O. Ponsler Memorial State Scenic Viewpoint

		Nearby Beach Access		Rating:	
Mgd by: State Parks				★★★☆☆	Astoria
Parking Lot: **small**		Pedestrian	**yes**		Seaside
" roadside – **a few**		Vehicle	**yes**		Tillamook
		Boat	no	Part of	Lincoln City
Drinking water	no			Washburne	Newport
Tables/benches	**yes**	Recreation		SP. Walk the	
Restrooms	no	Horse riding	no	¼ mile Hobbit	→ Florence
Camping	no	Tidepooling	no	Trail to the	Reedsport
Showers	no	WhaleWatching	no	beach, 0.8 mile	Coos Bay
Phone	no	Surfing	**yes**	north of Devil's	Bandon
Info Center	no	Bicycling	no	Elbow.	Port Orford
Fee	no	Hiking/trails	**yes**		Gold Beach
[Has a very nice creek]		Boating	no		Brookings

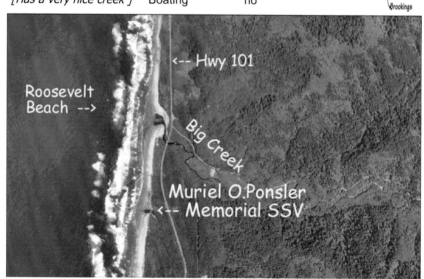

Aerial photo courtesy of U.S. Geological Survey, 27May94   ***Width is approx. 2 miles***

Off US 101, 15 miles north of Florence.

Carl G. Washburne Memorial State Park (The Day Use Area)

		Nearby Beach Access		Rating:
Mgd by: State Parks				
Parking Lot:	**large**	Pedestrian	**yes**	★★★☆☆
" roadside –	no	Vehicle	**yes**	
		Boat	no	1,089 acres
Drinking water	**yes**			
Tables/benches	**yes**	Recreation		Two miles on
Restrooms	**yes**	Horse riding	no	the beach to
Camping	no	Tidepooling	**yes**	Heceta Head
Showers	no	WhaleWatching	**yes**	Lighthouse.
Phone	no	Surfing	no	
Info Center	no	Bicycling	no	
Fee	no	Hiking/trails	**yes**	
[The campground has all facilities]		Boating	no	

Astoria
Seaside

Tillamook

Lincoln City

Newport

→ Florence

Reedsport

Coos Bay
Bandon

Port Orford

Gold Beach
Brookings

<-- Hwy 101

<-- campground

<-- parking & picnic area

<-- Blowout Creek

Carl G. Washburne
Memorial State Park

Aerial photo courtesy of U.S. Geological Survey, 27May94   **Width is approx. 2 miles**

Off US 101, 13 miles north of Florence, just north of Heceta Head.

Devil's Elbow State Park & Heceta Head Lighthouse SSV

Mgd by: State Parks		Nearby Beach Access		Rating:
Parking Lot:	**large**	Pedestrian	**yes**	★ ★ ★ ★ ☆
" roadside –	**yes**	Vehicle	**yes**	
		Boat	no	546 acres
Drinking water	**yes**			
Tables/benches	**yes**	Recreation		Strongest light
Restrooms	**yes**	Horse riding	no	on the coast;
Camping	no	Tidepooling	no	seen 21 miles
Showers	no	WhaleWatching	**yes**	out to sea. A
Phone	no	Surfing	no	B&B is located
Info Center	no	Bicycling	no	here in the old
Fee	**yes**	Hiking/trails	**yes**	Coast Guard
[Short trail to lighthouse]		Boating	no	building.

Astoria
Seaside
Tillamook
Lincoln City
Newport
→ Florence
Reedsport
Coos Bay
Bandon
Port Orford
Gold Beach
Brookings

<-- Hwy 101

<-- Heceta Head Lighthouse

<-- beach & picnic area

<-- Devil's Elbow   Cape Creek

Aerial photo courtesy of U.S. Geological Survey, 27May94   ***Width is approx. 2 miles***

Off US 101, 12 miles north of Florence.

Baker Beach Recreation Site

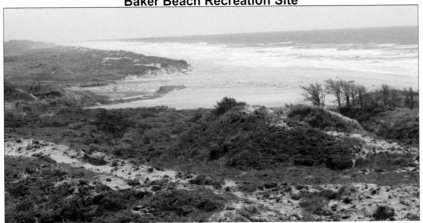

Mgd by:	USFS	Nearby Beach Access		Rating:
Parking Lot:	**small**	Pedestrian	**yes**	★ ★ ★ ☆ ☆
" roadside –	**a few**	Vehicle	**yes**	
		Boat	no	C & M Horse
Drinking water	**yes**			Stables
Tables/benches	**yes**	Recreation		nearby.
Restrooms	**yes**	Horse riding	**yes**	The dry sand
Camping	**yes**	Tidepooling	no	beach is
Showers	no	WhaleWatching	no	closed 3/15 –
Phone	no	Surfing	no	9/15 for Snowy
Info Center	no	Bicycling	no	Plover
Fee	**yes**	Hiking/trails	**yes**	nesting.
[Coast Horse Trail System]		Boating	no	

Astoria
Seaside
Tillamook
Lincoln City
Newport
→ Florence
Reedsport
Coos Bay
Bandon
Port Orford
Gold Beach
Brookings

<-- Lilly Lake & horse trails

Baker Beach -->

the road in

<-- Hwy 101

sand

Aerial photo courtesy of U.S. Geological Survey, 27May94   **Width is approx. 2 miles**

Off US 101, 5 ½ miles north of Florence, then ½ mile west.

Sutton Creek Recreation Site

		Nearby Beach Access		Rating:
Mgd by:	USFS			★ ★ ★ ☆ ☆
Parking Lot:	**medium**	Pedestrian	**yes**	
" roadside –	no	Vehicle	**yes**	
		Boat	no	Wetland, river;
Drinking water	**yes**			very photo
Tables/benches	**yes**	Recreation		worthy. You
Restrooms	**yes**	Horse riding	no	can hike
Camping	**yes**	Tidepooling	no	across the
Showers	no	WhaleWatching	no	creek to the
Phone	no	Surfing	no	ocean shore
Info Center	no	Bicycling	**yes**	from near the
Fee	**yes**	Hiking/trails	**yes**	observation
				deck.

Astoria
Seaside
Tillamook
Lincoln City
Newport
→ Florence
Reedsport
Coos Bay
Bandon
Port Orford
Gold Beach
Brookings

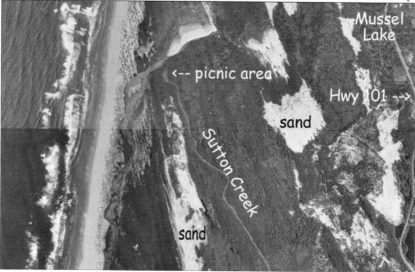

Aerial photo courtesy of U.S. Geological Survey, 27May94   **Width is approx. 2 miles**

Off US 101, 5 miles north of Florence.

Siuslaw North Jetty

Mgd by: Army Corps		Nearby Beach Access		Rating:
Parking Lot:	**large**	Pedestrian	**yes**	★ ★ ★ ☆ ☆
" roadside –	no	Vehicle	**yes**	
		Boat	no	This is quite a popular area. There is camping at nearby Lane County's Harbor Vista Park.
Drinking water	no			
Tables/benches	no	Recreation		
Restrooms	**yes**	Horse riding	no	
Camping	no	Tidepooling	no	
Showers	no	WhaleWatching	no	
Phone	no	Surfing	no	
Info Center	no	Bicycling	no	
Fee	no	Hiking/trails	no	
[Scuba diving]		Boating	no	

Astoria
Seaside
Tillamook
Lincoln City
Newport
→ Florence
Reedsport
Coos Bay
Bandon
Port Orford
Gold Beach
Brookings

Aerial photo courtesy of U.S. Geological Survey, 27May94   **Width is approx. 2 miles**

In Florence, turn west off Hwy 101 on N. 35th St., go 3.3 miles to end of the road.

South Jetty Road - Oregon Dunes NRA

		Nearby Beach Access		Rating:
Mgd by:	USFS			★ ★ ☆ ☆ ☆
Parking Lot:	**large**	Pedestrian	**yes**	
" roadside –	**yes**	Vehicle	**yes**	
		Boat	no	The Dunes
Drinking water	**yes**			cover 31,000
Tables/benches	no	Recreation		acres. This is a
Restrooms	**yes**	Horse riding	no	long, poor road
Camping	no	Tidepooling	no	with several
Showers	no	WhaleWatching	no	beach
Phone	no	Surfing	**yes**	accesses. The
Info Center	no	Bicycling	no	young crowd
Fee	**yes**	Hiking/trails	no	goes to the
[OHV's, crabbing, scuba]		Boating	no	road's end.

Astoria
Seaside
Tillamook
Lincoln City
Newport
→ Florence
Reedsport
Coos Bay
Bandon
Port Orford
Gold Beach
Brookings

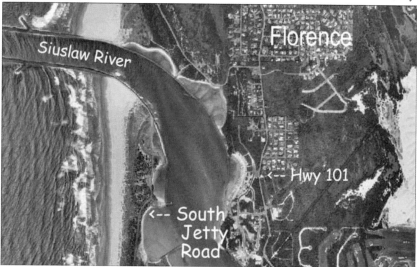

Aerial photo courtesy of U.S. Geological Survey, 27May94   **Width is approx. 2 miles**

Off US 101, ½ mile from south end of the bridge over the Siuslaw River.

Jessie M. Honeyman Memorial State Park

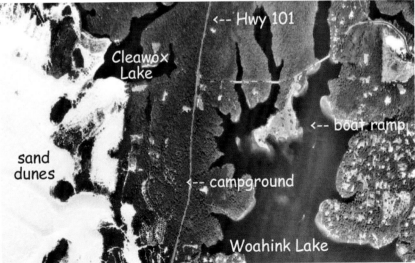

Mgd by:	State Parks	Nearby Beach Access		Rating:	Astoria
Parking Lot:	**many**	Pedestrian	no	★★★★☆	Seaside
" roadside –	no	Vehicle	no		Tillamook
		Boat	no	522 acres	Lincoln City
Drinking water	**yes**				Newport
Tables/benches	**yes**	Recreation		On both sides	
Restrooms	**yes**	Horse riding	no	of Hwy 101;	→ Florence
Camping	**yes**	Tidepooling	no	Cleawox and	Reedsport
Showers	**yes**	WhaleWatching	no	Woahink	Coos Bay
Phone	**yes**	Surfing	no	Lakes. Very	Bandon
Info Center	**yes**	Bicycling	**yes**	beach like, but	Port Orford
Fee	**yes**	Hiking/trails	**yes**	not on the	Gold Beach
[Kayaking, OHV's, dunes]		Boating	**yes**	ocean shore.	Brookings

Aerial photo courtesy of U.S. Geological Survey, 27May94   **Width is approx. 2 miles**

Off US 101, 3 miles south of Florence.

Siltcoos Beach - Oregon Dunes NRA

		Nearby Beach Access		Rating:	
Mgd by:	USFS			★ ★ ★ ☆ ☆	
Parking Lot:	**small**	Pedestrian	**yes**		
" roadside –	no	Vehicle	**yes**		
		Boat	no	ODNRA is	
Drinking water	**yes**			about 31,000	
Tables/benches	**yes**	Recreation		acres.	
Restrooms	**yes**	Horse riding	no	Day use area	
Camping	**yes**	Tidepooling	no	has few	
Showers	no	WhaleWatching	no	facilities.	
Phone	no	Surfing	no	OHV's allowed	
Info Center	no	Bicycling	no	some places.	
Fee	**yes**	Hiking/trails	**yes**	There are two	
[Canoeing on the Siltcoos]		Boating	**yes**	campgrounds.	

Astoria
Seaside
Tillamook
Lincoln City
Newport
Florence →
Reedsport
Coos Bay
Bandon
Port Orford
Gold Beach
Brookings

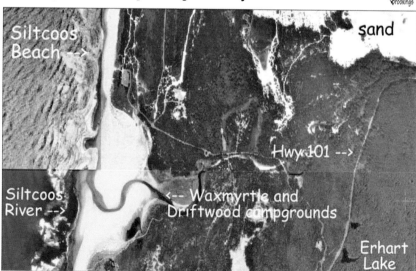

Aerial photo courtesy of U.S. Geological Survey, 27May94   ***Width is approx. 2 miles***

Off US 101, 8 miles south of Florence.

Sparrow Park - Oregon Dunes NRA

Mgd by:	USFS	Nearby Beach Access		Rating:	Astoria
Parking Lot:	**small**	Pedestrian	**yes**	★ ★ ★ ☆ ☆	Seaside
" roadside –	**a few**	Vehicle	**yes**		Tillamook
		Boat	no	3.9 mile good	Lincoln City
Drinking water	no			gravel road	Newport
Tables/benches	no	Recreation		from US 101 to	Florence
Restrooms	no	Horse riding	no	parking lot.	Reedsport
Camping	no	Tidepooling	no	About as	Coos Bay
Showers	no	WhaleWatching	no	isolated as any	Bandon
Phone	no	Surfing	**yes**	place in this	Port Orford
Info Center	no	Bicycling	no	book. Sign at	Gold Beach
Fee	no	Hiking/trails	**yes**	top of hill on	Brookings
[Beach combing, surf fishing]		Boating	no	US 101.	

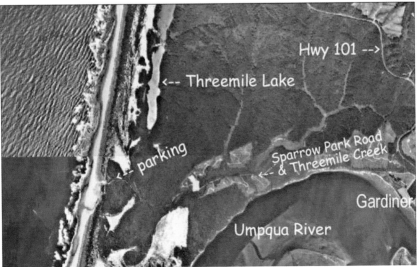

Hwy 101 -->

<-- Threemile Lake

<-- parking

Sparrow Park Road & Threemile Creek

Gardiner

Umpqua River

Aerial photo courtesy of U.S. Geological Survey, 27May94 **Width is approx. 2 miles**

Off US 101, 1½ miles north of Gardiner, 4 miles north of Reedsport.

Umpqua Lighthouse State Park

		Nearby Beach Access		Rating:
Mgd by:	State Parks	Pedestrian	yes	★ ★ ★ ★ ☆
Parking Lot:	**many**	Vehicle	yes	
" roadside –	no	Boat	no	450 acres
Drinking water	**yes**			Lighthouse
Tables/benches	**yes**	Recreation		and museum.
Restrooms	**yes**	Horse riding	no	Whales come
Camping	**yes**	Tidepooling	no	right to the
Showers	**yes**	WhaleWatching	yes	river's mouth.
Phone	**yes**	Surfing	no	Three beach
Info Center	no	Bicycling	no	access parking
Fee	**yes**	Hiking/trails	yes	areas.
[Big OHV country]		Boating	yes	

Astoria
Seaside
Tillamook
Lincoln City
Newport
Florence
→ Reedsport
Coos Bay
Bandon
Port Orford
Gold Beach
Brookings

Aerial photo courtesy of U.S. Geological Survey, 27May94   **Width is approx. 2 miles**

Off US 101, 6 miles south of Reedsport; enter through Salmon Harbor.

Horsfall Beach

		Nearby Beach Access		Rating:	
Mgd by:	USFS	<u>Nearby Beach Access</u>		★ ★ ☆ ☆ ☆	
Parking Lot: **medium**		Pedestrian	**yes**		
" roadside –	no	Vehicle	**yes**		
		Boat	no	Very popular	
Drinking water	**yes**			with OHV'ers.	
Tables/benches	no	<u>Recreation</u>		Named for a	
Restrooms	**yes**	Horse riding	**yes**	Dr. Horsfall,	
Camping	**yes**	Tidepooling	no	not a horse fall.	
Showers	no	WhaleWatching	no	This area is	
Phone	**yes**	Surfing	no	packed with	
Info Center	no	Bicycling	no	people on holi-	
Fee	no	Hiking/trails	**yes**	days.	
[Horse trails to the south]		Boating	no		

Astoria
Seaside
Tillamook
Lincoln City
Newport
Florence
Reedsport
→ Coos Bay
Bandon
Port Orford
Gold Beach
Brookings

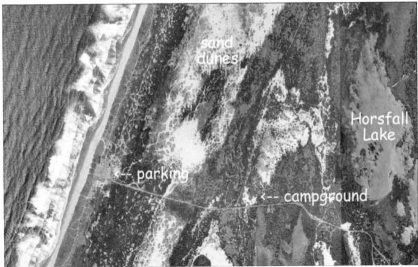

sand dunes

Horsfall Lake

<-- parking

<-- campground

Aerial photo courtesy of U.S. Geological Survey, 27May94   **Width is approx. 2 miles**

Off US 101, 5 miles north of Coos Bay.

Bastendorf Beach

		Nearby Beach Access		Rating:	Astoria
Mgd by: Coos County				★ ★ ★ ☆ ☆	Seaside
Parking Lot: **medium**		Pedestrian	**yes**		
" roadside –	**yes**	Vehicle	**yes**		Tillamook
		Boat	no	91 acres	Lincoln City
Drinking water	no				Newport
Tables/benches	no	Recreation		A popular,	
Restrooms	**yes**	Horse riding	no	nearby county	Florence
Camping	no	Tidepooling	no	campground	Reedsport
Showers	no	WhaleWatching	no	has all	
Phone	no	Surfing	**yes**	facilities.	→ Coos Bay
Info Center	no	Bicycling	no		Bandon
Fee	no	Hiking/trails	no		Port Orford
[Very good for kite flying]		Boating	no		Gold Beach
					Brookings

South Jetty -->

Coos Bay

Bastendorf Beach -->

Yoakam Point -->

<-- County Park

Cape Arago Hwy

Aerial photo courtesy of U.S. Geological Survey, 27May94   ***Width is approx. 2 miles***

Ten miles west of Coos Bay, on the Cape Arago Highway.

Sunset Bay State Park

		Nearby Beach Access		Rating:	
Mgd by:	State Parks			★ ★ ★ ★ ☆	Astoria
Parking Lot:	**many**	Pedestrian	**yes**		Seaside
" roadside –	no	Vehicle	**yes**		Tillamook
		Boat	**yes**	395 acres	Lincoln City
Drinking water	**yes**				Newport
Tables/benches	**yes**	Recreation		Swimming,	Florence
Restrooms	**yes**	Horse riding	no	scuba diving,	Reedsport
Camping	**yes**	Tidepooling	**yes**	surf fishing,	
Showers	**yes**	WhaleWatching	no	kayaking.	→ Coos Bay
Phone	**yes**	Surfing	**yes**	Elephant seals,	Bandon
Info Center	**yes**	Bicycling	**yes**	sea lions on	Port Orford
Fee	**yes**	Hiking/trails	**yes**	offshore reef.	Gold Beach
[Very sheltered ocean cove]		Boating	**yes**		Brookings

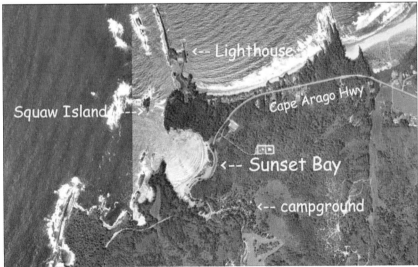

Aerial photo courtesy of U.S. Geological Survey, 27May94   **Width is approx. 2 miles**

Twelve miles southwest of Coos Bay, on the Cape Arago Highway.

Shore Acres State Park and Botanical Gardens

Mgd by: State Parks	Nearby Beach Access		Rating:
Parking Lot: **many**	Pedestrian	**yes**	★ ★ ★ ★ ☆
" roadside – no	Vehicle	**yes**	
	Boat	no	743 acres
Drinking water **yes**			
Tables/benches **yes**	Recreation		There is an
Restrooms **yes**	Horse riding	no	access path to
Camping no	Tidepooling	no	Simpson
Showers no	WhaleWatching	**yes**	Beach. Lots of
Phone **yes**	Surfing	no	wave action
Info Center **yes**	Bicycling	no	here. Famous
Fee **yes**	Hiking/trails	**yes**	botanical
[Has a wave watching shelter] Boating		no	gardens.

Astoria
Seaside
Tillamook
Lincoln City
Newport
Florence
Reedsport
→ Coos Bay
Bandon
Port Orford
Gold Beach
Brookings

Botanical Gardens -->   <-- parking

Cape Arago Hwy

<-- Sea Lion Viewpoint

Aerial photo courtesy of U.S. Geological Survey, 27May94   **Width is approx. 2 miles**

Thirteen miles southwest of Coos Bay, on the Cape Arago Highway.

Cape Arago State Park

		Nearby Beach Access		Rating:		
Mgd by:	State Parks			★ ★ ★ ☆ ☆		Astoria / Seaside
Parking Lot:	**medium**	Pedestrian	**yes**			
" roadside –	**yes**	Vehicle	**yes**			Tillamook
		Boat	no	134 acres		
						Lincoln City
Drinking water	no					Newport
Tables/benches	**yes**	Recreation		Cape Arago		
Restrooms	**yes**	Horse riding	no	Lighthouse not		Florence
Camping	no	Tidepooling	**yes**	open to public.		Reedsport
Showers	no	WhaleWatching	**yes**	Seals and sea		
Phone	no	Surfing	no	lions on nearby	→	Coos Bay / Bandon
Info Center	no	Bicycling	no	Simpson (the		Port Orford
Fee	no	Hiking/trails	**yes**	timber baron)		Gold Beach
[Trails to the inter-tidal area]		Boating	no	Reef.		Brookings

Shell Island-->

North Cove

Cape Arago -->

Drake Point -->

South Cove

Aerial photo courtesy of U.S. Geological Survey, 27May94   **Width is approx. 2 miles**

Fourteen miles southwest of Coos Bay, on the Cape Arago Highway.

Seven Devils State Recreation Site

		Nearby Beach Access		Rating:
Mgd by:	State Parks			★★★☆☆
Parking Lot:	**large**	Pedestrian	**yes**	
" roadside –	**yes**	Vehicle	**yes**	
		Boat	no	Two miles of
Drinking water	no			good beach.
Tables/benches	**yes**	Recreation		Used to have
Restrooms	**yes**	Horse riding	no	water but the
Camping	no	Tidepooling	no	pipes rusted
Showers	no	WhaleWatching	no	out.
Phone	no	Surfing	**yes**	
Info Center	no	Bicycling	**yes**	
Fee	no	Hiking/trails	**yes**	
		Boating	no	

Astoria
Seaside
Tillamook
Lincoln City
Newport
Florence
Reedsport
→ Coos Bay
Bandon
Port Orford
Gold Beach
Brookings

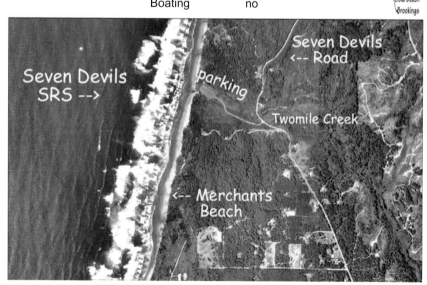

Aerial photo courtesy of U.S. Geological Survey, 27May94   **Width is approx. 2 miles**

Ten miles north of Bandon on Seven Devils Highway.

Whiskey Run - Seven Devils State Recreation Site

Mgd by: State Parks	Nearby Beach Access		Rating:	
Parking Lot: **small**	Pedestrian	**yes**	★★★☆☆	
" roadside – no	Vehicle	**yes**		
	Boat	no	Driving on the	
Drinking water no			beach is OK.	
Tables/benches **yes**	Recreation		Rules are	
Restrooms **yes**	Horse riding	no	posted.	
Camping no	Tidepooling	no		
Showers no	WhaleWatching	no		
Phone no	Surfing	**yes**		
Info Center no	Bicycling	**yes**		
Fee no	Hiking/trails	**yes**		
[Not visited much]	Boating	no		

Aerial photo courtesy of U.S. Geological Survey, 27May94   ***Width is approx. 2 miles***

Nine miles north of Bandon, on Seven Devils Highway.

Bullards Beach State Park

		Nearby Beach Access		Rating:	
Mgd by:	State Parks			★ ★ ★ ★ ★	Astoria
Parking Lot:	**many**	Pedestrian	**yes**		Seaside
" roadside –	**yes**	Vehicle	**yes**		Tillamook
		Boat	no	1,289 acres	Lincoln City
Drinking water	**yes**				Newport
Tables/benches	**yes**	Recreation		Campground is	
Restrooms	**yes**	Horse riding	**yes**	open year-	Florence
Camping	**yes**	Tidepooling	no	round.	Reedsport
Showers	**yes**	WhaleWatching	no	You can walk	
Phone	**yes**	Surfing	no	on the beach	Coos Bay
Info Center	**yes**	Bicycling	**yes**	north ½ mile to	Bandon
Fee	**yes**	Hiking/trails	**yes**	Whiskey Run.	Port Orford
[Has a horse camping area]		Boating	**yes**		Gold Beach
					Brookings

→ (arrow pointing to Bandon)

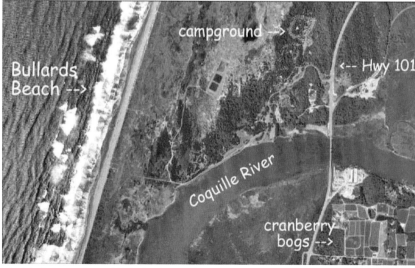

campground -->

Bullards Beach -->

<-- Hwy 101

Coquille River

cranberry bogs -->

Aerial photo courtesy of U.S. Geological Survey, 27May94   ***Width is approx. 2 miles***

Off US 101, 2 miles north of Bandon.

90

Coquille River Lighthouse - Bullards Beach SP

			Nearby Beach Access		Rating:	
Mgd by:	State Parks		Pedestrian	**yes**	★ ★ ★ ☆ ☆	
Parking Lot:	**large**		Vehicle	**yes**		
" roadside –	**a few**		Boat	no	Open for tours	
					daily May-	
Drinking water	no				October, week-	
Tables/benches	no		Recreation		ends in April.	
Restrooms	**yes**		Horse riding	no	Located in the	
Camping	no		Tidepooling	no	state park.	
Showers	no		WhaleWatching	no		
Phone	no		Surfing	no		
Info Center	no		Bicycling	no		
Fee	no		Hiking/trails	no		
[Solar-powered system]			Boating	no		

Aerial photo courtesy of U.S. Geological Survey, 27May94   **Width is approx. 2 miles**

Off US 101, 2 miles north of Bandon.

South Jetty County Park

Mgd by: Coos County

Parking Lot: **large**
" roadside – **yes**

Drinking water no
Tables/benches no
Restrooms **yes**
Camping no
Showers no
Phone no
Info Center no
Fee no
[Popular kite flying area]

Nearby Beach Access

Pedestrian	**yes**
Vehicle	**yes**
Boat	no

Recreation

Horse riding	no
Tidepooling	no
WhaleWatching	no
Surfing	no
Bicycling	no
Hiking/trails	no
Boating	no

Rating:
★ ★ ☆ ☆ ☆

Area tends to be rather congested and has a very commercial feeling to it.

Astoria
Seaside
Tillamook
Lincoln City
Newport
Florence
Reedsport
Coos Bay
→ Bandon
Port Orford
Gold Beach
Brookings

South Jetty County Park→

Coquille River

Bandon

Aerial photo courtesy of U.S. Geological Survey, 27May94   ***Width is approx. 2 miles***

At the harbor in Bandon.

Face Rock State Scenic Viewpoint and Kronenberg County Park

		Nearby Beach Access		Rating:
Mgd by: State-County-City		Pedestrian	**yes**	★ ★ ★ ☆ ☆
Parking Lot: **several**		Vehicle	**yes**	
areas for parking.		Boat	no	893 acres
Drinking water	**yes**			There are
Tables/benches	**yes**	Recreation		l-o-n-g steps at
Restrooms	**yes**	Horse riding	**yes**	the north end
Camping	no	Tidepooling	**yes**	to the beach.
Showers	no	WhaleWatching	**yes**	Several access
Phone	no	Surfing	no	points.
Info Center	no	Bicycling	no	
Fee	no	Hiking/trails	**yes**	
[This is cranberry country]		Boating	no	

Astoria
Seaside
Tillamook
Lincoln City
Newport
Florence
Reedsport
Coos Bay
→ Bandon
Port Orford
Gold Beach
Brookings

Coquille Point -->

Bandon

Face Rock -->

<-- Bandon Ocean Wayside

Aerial photo courtesy of U.S. Geological Survey, 27May94   **Width is approx. 2 miles**

One mile southwest of Bandon on Beach Loop Drive.

Beach Loop Drive - Bandon State Natural Area

		Nearby Beach Access		Rating:	
Mgd by:	State Parks	Pedestrian	**yes**	★ ★ ★ ☆ ☆	
Parking Lot:	several	Vehicle	**yes**		
	lots on the drive.	Boat	no	893 acres	
Drinking water	no				
Tables/benches	**yes**	Recreation		You can hike	
Restrooms	**yes**	Horse riding	no	south on the	
Camping	no	Tidepooling	**yes**	beach 8½	
Showers	no	WhaleWatching	no	miles to	
Phone	no	Surfing	no	Fourmile	
Info Center	no	Bicycling	no	Creek.	
Fee	no	Hiking/trails	**yes**		
[There are three waysides]		Boating	no		

Astoria
Seaside
Tillamook
Lincoln City
Newport
Florence
Reedsport
Coos Bay
→ Bandon
Port Orford
Gold Beach
Brookings

Devil's→
Kitchen

Bandon

<-- Beach Loop Drive

picnic
area

<-- cranberry bogs

Aerial photo courtesy of U.S. Geological Survey, 27May94 **Width is approx. 2 miles**

On Bandon Beach Loop Drive, 5 miles south of Bandon.

Cape Blanco State Park

		Nearby Beach Access		Rating:	
Mgd by:	State Parks			★ ★ ★ ★ ☆	Astoria
Parking Lot:	**medium**	Pedestrian	**yes**		Seaside
" roadside –	no	Vehicle	**yes**		Tillamook
		Boat	no	1,880 acres	Lincoln City
Drinking water	**yes**				Newport
Tables/benches	**yes**	Recreation		Road to beach	
Restrooms	**yes**	Horse riding	**yes**	is via the	Florence
Camping	**yes**	Tidepooling	**yes**	campground.	Reedsport
Showers	**yes**	WhaleWatching	**yes**	Windiest,	Coos Bay
Phone	**yes**	Surfing	no	westernmost	Bandon
Info Center	no	Bicycling	no	point on the	→ Port Orford
Fee	**yes**	Hiking/trails	**yes**	Oregon coast.	Gold Beach
[Lighthouse tours Apr-Oct]		Boating	**yes**	100 mph gales.	Brookings

Aerial photo courtesy of U.S. Geological Survey, 27May94 **Width is approx. 2 miles**

Nine miles north of Port Orford and 3 miles west from Hwy 101.

Paradise Point State Recreation Site

		Nearby Beach Access		Rating:
Mgd by:	State Parks	Pedestrian	**yes**	★ ★ ☆ ☆ ☆
Parking Lot:	**medium**	Vehicle	**yes**	
" roadside –	no	Boat	no	Sometimes
				known as
Drinking water	no	Recreation		Garrison
Tables/benches	no	Horse riding	no	Beach
Restrooms	no	Tidepooling	no	Wayside.
Camping	no	WhaleWatching	no	Private homes
Showers	no	Surfing	no	close by.
Phone	no	Bicycling	no	
Info Center	no	Hiking/trails	no	
Fee	no	Boating	no	
[Many offshore rocks]				

Astoria
Seaside
Tillamook
Lincoln City
Newport
Florence
Reedsport
Coos Bay
Bandon
→ Port Orford
Gold Beach
Brookings

Paradise
Point SRS →

Hwy 101 →

Paradise Point Road

Garrison Lake

Aerial photo courtesy of U.S. Geological Survey, 27May94   **Width is approx. 2 miles**

One mile north of Port Orford, then one mile west from Hwy 101.

Agate Beach Wayside

Mgd by:	State Parks	Nearby Beach Access		Rating:
Parking Lot:	**large**	Pedestrian	**yes**	★ ★ ☆ ☆ ☆
" roadside –	no	Vehicle	**yes**	
		Boat	no	An old RV park
Drinking water	no			was purchased
Tables/benches	**yes**	Recreation		by the State in
Restrooms	**yes**	Horse riding	no	2003. 250
Camping	no	Tidepooling	no	yards on good
Showers	no	WhaleWatching	no	trail to a coarse
Phone	no	Surfing	no	sand beach.
Info Center	no	Bicycling	no	
Fee	no	Hiking/trails	no	

Astoria
Seaside
Tillamook
Lincoln City
Newport
Florence
Reedsport
Coos Bay
Bandon
→ Port Orford
Gold Beach
Brookings

[Access is thru an old RV park] Boating **nearby**

Agate Beach -->

Port Orford

Klooqueh Rock

harbor
dock

The Heads -->

Aerial photo courtesy of U.S. Geological Survey, 27May94　　**Width is approx. 2 miles**

In north Port Orford, take 12ᵗʰ St. to the west from Hwy 101.

Battle Rock City Park

		Nearby Beach Access		Rating:	
Mgd by: Port Orford				★ ★ ★ ☆ ☆	Astoria
Parking Lot: **medium**		Pedestrian	**yes**		Seaside
" roadside –	no	Vehicle	**yes**		Tillamook
		Boat	no	Although right	Lincoln City
Drinking water	**yes**			in town, there	Newport
Tables/benches	**yes**	Recreation		are good,	
Restrooms	**yes**	Horse riding	no	easily	Florence
Camping	no	Tidepooling	no	accessible	Reedsport
Showers	no	WhaleWatching	**yes**	beaches for	Coos Bay
Phone	no	Surfing	**yes**	walking to both	Bandon
Info Center	no	Bicycling	no	the north and	→ Port Orford
Fee	no	Hiking/trails	**yes**	to the south.	Gold Beach
[Interpretive signs]		Boating	no		Brookings

Aerial photo courtesy of U.S. Geological Survey, 27May94   **Width is approx. 2 miles**

In Port Orford.

Hubbard Creek - Humbug Mountain State Park

		Nearby Beach Access		Rating:	
Mgd by:	State Parks	Pedestrian	**yes**	★ ★ ★ ☆ ☆	
Parking Lot:	no	Vehicle	**yes**		
" roadside – **several**		Boat	no	Humbug SP is	
				1,842 acres	
Drinking water	no				
Tables/benches	no	Recreation			
Restrooms	no	Horse riding	no	There is	
Camping	no	Tidepooling	no	access to a	
Showers	no	WhaleWatching	no	beautiful, long	
Phone	no	Surfing	**yes**	cove beach. A	
Info Center	no	Bicycling	no	short, easy	
Fee	no	Hiking/trails	no	hike.	
[Many surfers come here]		Boating	no		

Astoria
Seaside
Tillamook
Lincoln City
Newport
Florence
Reedsport
Coos Bay
Bandon
→ Port Orford
Gold Beach
Brookings

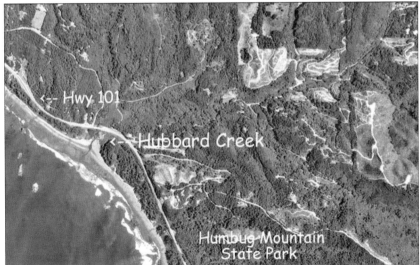

Aerial photo courtesy of U.S. Geological Survey, 27May94   **Width is approx. 2 miles**

Off US 101, one mile south of Port Orford.

Humbug Mountain State Park

		Nearby Beach Access		Rating:	
Mgd by:	State Parks			★ ★ ★ ☆ ☆	
Parking Lot:	**many**	Pedestrian	**yes**		
" roadside –	**yes**	Vehicle	**yes**	1,842 acres	
		Boat	no		
Drinking water	**yes**				
Tables/benches	**yes**	Recreation		5½ mile trail to	
Restrooms	**yes**	Horse riding	no	top of the	
Camping	**yes**	Tidepooling	no	mountain.	
Showers	**yes**	WhaleWatching	no	Elevation gain	
Phone	**yes**	Surfing	no	is 1,730 feet.	
Info Center	**yes**	Bicycling	**yes**	Special parking	
Fee	**yes**	Hiking/trails	**yes**	lot for the	
[Great camping, OK beach]		Boating	no	trailhead.	

Astoria
Seaside
Tillamook
Lincoln City
Newport
Florence
Reedsport
Coos Bay
Bandon
Port Orford →
Gold Beach
Brookings

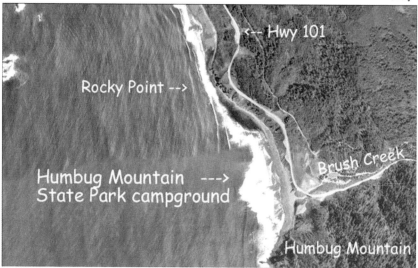

Aerial photo courtesy of U.S. Geological Survey, 27May94   **Width is approx. 2 miles**

Off US 101, 6 miles south of Port Orford.

Arizona Beach - Mussel Creek

Mgd by:	OPRD	
Parking Lot:	private	
" roadside –	no	

Drinking water	n/a
Tables/benches	n/a
Restrooms	n/a
Camping	n/a
Showers	n/a
Phone	n/a
Info Center	n/a
Fee	n/a
[OK if you're in an RV]	

Nearby Beach Access

Pedestrian	**yes**
Vehicle	**yes**
Boat	no

Recreation

Horse riding	n/a
Tidepooling	n/a
WhaleWatching	n/a
Surfing	n/a
Bicycling	n/a
Hiking/trails	n/a
Boating	n/a

Rating:
★ ★ ☆ ☆ ☆

Only access is through an RV park that is rather large; has oceanfront RV spaces.

Astoria
Seaside
Tillamook
Lincoln City
Newport
Florence
Reedsport
Coos Bay
Bandon
Port Orford
→ Gold Beach
Brookings

Arizona Beach -->
Mussel Creek -->
Myrtle Creek
Hwy 101 -->

Aerial photo courtesy of U.S. Geological Survey, 27May94   **Width is approx. 2 miles**

Off US 101, about 11 miles north of Gold Beach.

Ophir Beach

Mgd by: State Parks	Nearby Beach Access		Rating:
Parking Lot: **medium**	Pedestrian	**yes**	★ ★ ★ ☆ ☆
" roadside – no	Vehicle	**yes**	
	Boat	no	A well-used
Drinking water **yes**			rest area, but
Tables/benches **yes**	Recreation		the beach itself
Restrooms **yes**	Horse riding	no	is usually
Camping no	Tidepooling	no	rather empty.
Showers no	WhaleWatching	no	Especially
Phone **yes**	Surfing	no	worth a stop
Info Center no	Bicycling	no	when on a trip
Fee no	Hiking/trails	no	with the kids.
	Boating	no	

Astoria
Seaside

Tillamook

Lincoln City

Newport

Florence

Reedsport

Coos Bay
Bandon

Port Orford

→ Gold Beach

Brookings

Aerial photo courtesy of U.S. Geological Survey, 27May94 **Width is approx. 2 miles**

Off US 101, 9½ miles north of Gold Beach.

Nesika Beach

Mgd by: Curry County

Parking Lot:	no
" roadside –	**yes**
Drinking water	no
Tables/benches	no
Restrooms	no
Camping	no
Showers	no
Phone	no
Info Center	no
Fee	no

Nearby Beach Access

Pedestrian	**yes**
Vehicle	**yes**
Boat	no

Recreation

Horse riding	no
Tidepooling	no
WhaleWatching	no
Surfing	no
Bicycling	no
Hiking/trails	no
Boating	no

Rating:
★ ★ ★ ☆ ☆

Parking is at the far north end of the town area. A beach mostly used by the locals. Humbug Mountain in the distance.

Astoria
Seaside
Tillamook
Lincoln City
Newport
Florence
Reedsport
Coos Bay
Bandon
Port Orford
→ Gold Beach
Brookings

<-- Hwy 101

Nesika Beach -->

Nesika Beach

Aerial photo courtesy of U.S. Geological Survey, 27May94   ***Width is approx. 2 miles***

Turn west off US 101 to the town, about 8 miles north of Gold Beach.

Otter Point State Recreation Site - Bailey Beach

Mgd by: State Parks

Parking Lot: **small**
" roadside – **a few**

Drinking water   no
Tables/benches   no
Restrooms   no
Camping   no
Showers   no
Phone   no
Info Center   no
Fee   no
[Interesting offshore rocks]

Nearby Beach Access

Pedestrian   **yes**
Vehicle   **yes**
Boat   no

Recreation
Horse riding   no
Tidepooling   no
WhaleWatching   no
Surfing   no
Bicycling   no
Hiking/trails   no
Boating   no

Rating:
★☆☆☆☆

Nice, but beach is not very easily accessible. Steep "hidden" trail at north end of parking lot. Use Old Coast Road from US 101.

Astoria
Seaside
Tillamook
Lincoln City
Newport
Florence
Reedsport
Coos Bay
Bandon
Port Orford
→ Gold Beach
Brookings

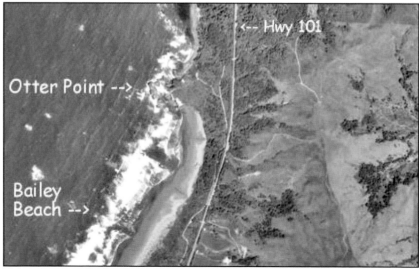

<-- Hwy 101

Otter Point -->

Bailey Beach -->

Aerial photo courtesy of U.S. Geological Survey, 27May94   **Width is approx. 2 miles**

Off US 101, 4 miles north of Gold Beach.

Doyle Point and Hi-Tide Lane

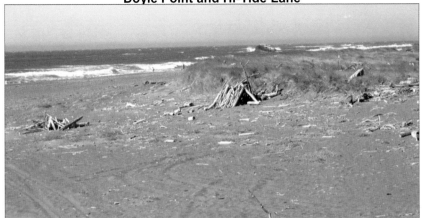

		Nearby Beach Access		Rating:
Mgd by:	Army Corps	_Nearby Beach Access_		★☆☆☆☆
Parking Lot:	**large**	Pedestrian	**yes**	
" roadside	no	Vehicle	**yes**	
		Boat	no	Area shows
Drinking water	no			hard use. Lots
Tables/benches	no	_Recreation_		of empty
Restrooms	no	Horse riding	**yes**	space; come
Camping	no	Tidepooling	no	with your dogs
Showers	no	WhaleWatching	no	and horses!
Phone	no	Surfing	no	
Info Center	no	Bicycling	no	
Fee	no	Hiking/trails	no	
		Boating	no	

Aerial photo courtesy of U.S. Geological Survey, 27May94   **Width is approx. 2 miles**

Off US 101, 1 mile from north end of the bridge over the Rogue River.

South Jetty of the Rogue River and Airport Beach (Gold Beach)

		Nearby Beach Access		Rating:
Mgd by: Port Authority				★ ★ ☆ ☆ ☆
Parking Lot:	**large**	Pedestrian	**yes**	
" roadside –	**yes**	Vehicle	**yes**	
		Boat	no	Minimally
Drinking water	no			maintained
Tables/benches	no	Recreation		area. Park
Restrooms	**yes***	Horse riding	**yes**	anywhere on
Camping	no	Tidepooling	no	the roadside
Showers	no	WhaleWatching	no	and walk to the
Phone	no	Surfing	no	beach. Check
Info Center	no	Bicycling	no	out the Sailors-
Fee	no	Hiking/trails	no	lost-at-sea
[In lot behind Post Office]*		Boating	**nearby**	Memorial.

Astoria
Seaside
Tillamook
Lincoln City
Newport
Florence
Reedsport
Coos Bay
Bandon
Port Orford
→ Gold Beach
Brookings

Aerial photo courtesy of U.S. Geological Survey, 27May94   **Width is approx. 2 miles**

At Gold Beach, in the harbor area.

Curry County Fairgrounds and South Beach Park

Mgd by: Curry County
Parking Lot: **2 large**
  " roadside –   no

Drinking water no
Tables/benches **yes**
Restrooms **yes**
Camping no
Showers no
Phone no
Info Center no
Fee no
[South Beach often is empty]

Nearby Beach Access	
Pedestrian	yes
Vehicle	yes
Boat	no

Recreation	
Horse riding	yes
Tidepooling	no
WhaleWatching	no
Surfing	no
Bicycling	no
Hiking/trails	no
Boating	no

Rating:
★ ★ ★ ☆ ☆

Horseback riding is popular; drive around to the back of the fairgrounds for picnic tables, beach access.

Astoria
Seaside
Tillamook
Lincoln City
Newport
Florence
Reedsport
Coos Bay
Bandon
Port Orford
→ Gold Beach
Brookings

Curry County Fairgrounds --->

South Beach -->

<-- Hwy 101

<-> parking

Aerial photo courtesy of U.S. Geological Survey, 27May94   **Width is approx. 2 miles**

South Beach Park is at the very south end of Gold Beach.

Buena Vista Beach

Mgd by: State Parks
Parking Lot: **large**
" roadside – no

Drinking water no
Tables/benches no
Restrooms no
Camping no
Showers no
Phone no
Info Center no
Fee no

<u>Nearby Beach Access</u>
Pedestrian **yes**
Vehicle **yes**
Boat no

<u>Recreation</u>
Horse riding no
Tidepooling no
WhaleWatching no
Surfing no
Bicycling no
Hiking/trails no
Boating no

Rating:
★★★☆☆

Broad, very
expansive
beaches.
Seems little
used
considering
how easy it is
to get to.

Astoria
Seaside
Tillamook
Lincoln City
Newport
Florence
Reedsport
Coos Bay
Bandon
Port Orford
→ Gold Beach
Brookings

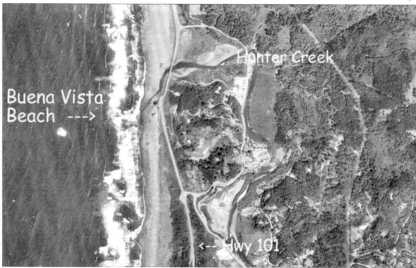

Buena Vista Beach --->

Hunter Creek

<-- Hwy 101

Aerial photo courtesy of U.S. Geological Survey, 27May94   **Width is approx. 2 miles**

Off US 101, 4 miles south of Gold Beach.

Cape Sebastian State Scenic Corridor

Mgd by: State Parks	Nearby Beach Access		Rating:	Astoria
Parking Lot: **many**	Pedestrian	**yes**	★★★★☆	Seaside
" roadside – no	Vehicle	**yes**		Tillamook
	Boat	no	1,104 acres	Lincoln City
Drinking water no				Newport
Tables/benches no	Recreation		Southern part	
Restrooms **yes**	Horse riding	no	has the good	Florence
Camping no	Tidepooling	no	beaches.	Reedsport
Showers no	WhaleWatching	**yes**	Oregon Coast	Coos Bay
Phone no	Surfing	no	Trail goes	Bandon
Info Center no	Bicycling	no	across the	Port Orford
Fee no	Hiking/trails	**yes**	cape.	Gold Beach
[1½ mile trail to Cape's tip] Boating		no		Brookings

Cape Sebastian

Hunters Cove and Island -->

<-- Hwy 101

Aerial photo courtesy of U.S. Geological Survey, 27May94   **Width is approx. 2 miles**

Off US 101, 5 miles south of Gold Beach.

Myers Creek - Pistol River State Scenic Viewpoint

Mgd by: State Parks
Parking Lot: **medium**
  " roadside –   no

Drinking water	no
Tables/benches	no
Restrooms	no
Camping	no
Showers	no
Phone	no
Info Center	no
Fee	no

[Several access points]

<u>Nearby Beach Access</u>

Pedestrian	**yes**
Vehicle	**yes**
Boat	no

<u>Recreation</u>

Horse riding	no
Tidepooling	no
WhaleWatching	no
Surfing	no
Bicycling	no
Hiking/trails	no
Boating	no

Rating:
★ ★ ★ ☆ ☆

Pistol River SP
is 440 acres.

Beaches north
and south are
very long, and
are very easy
to get to.

Astoria
Seaside

Tillamook

Lincoln City
Newport

Florence

Reedsport

Coos Bay
Bandon

Port Orford

→ Gold Beach
Brookings

Hunters Cove   <-- Hwy 101

Hunters Island

Meyers Creek -->

Aerial photo courtesy of U.S. Geological Survey, 27May94   **Width is approx. 2 miles**

Off US 101, 7½ miles south of Gold Beach.

Pistol River State Scenic Viewpoint

Mgd by: State Parks	Nearby Beach Access		Rating:		Astoria
Parking Lot: **2 large**	Pedestrian	**yes**	★ ★ ★ ☆ ☆		Seaside
" roadside – no	Vehicle	**yes**			Tillamook
	Boat	no	Pistol River SP		Lincoln City
Drinking water no			is 440 acres.		Newport
Tables/benches **yes**	Recreation				Florence
Restrooms **yes**	Horse riding	**yes**	Very wide		Reedsport
Camping no	Tidepooling	no	beaches; one		Coos Bay
Showers no	WhaleWatching	no	of the most		Bandon
Phone no	Surfing	**yes**	popular surfing		Port Orford
Info Center no	Bicycling	no	spots, wind		Gold Beach
Fee no	Hiking/trails	**yes**	and board.	→	Brookings
[Ocean-carved-up beach]	Boating	no			

Pistol River
State Park

Pistol River

Aerial photo courtesy of U.S. Geological Survey, 27May94   **Width is approx. 2 miles**

Off US 101, 10 miles south of Gold Beach.

111

Arch Rock Viewpoint - Samuel H. Boardman SSC

		Nearby Beach Access		Rating:	
Mgd by:	State Parks			★ ★ ☆ ☆ ☆	→ Astoria / Seaside
Parking Lot:	**large**	Pedestrian	**yes**		
" roadside –	no	Vehicle	**yes**		Tillamook
		Boat	no	Boardman is	Lincoln City
Drinking water	no			1,471 acres.	Newport
Tables/benches	**yes**	Recreation			Florence
Restrooms	**yes**	Horse riding	no	No beach	Reedsport
Camping	no	Tidepooling	no	access here	
Showers	no	WhaleWatching	no	but it's	Coos Bay
Phone	no	Surfing	no	Included	Bandon
Info Center	no	Bicycling	no	because it's so	Port Orford
Fee	no	Hiking/trails	no	pleasant and	Gold Beach
[Good spot for lunch]		Boating	no	scenic.	Brookings

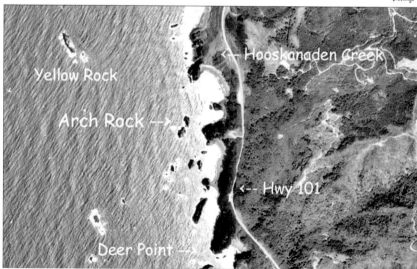

Yellow Rock

Arch Rock -->

<-- Hooskanaden Creek

<-- Hwy 101

Deer Point -->

Aerial photo courtesy of U.S. Geological Survey, 27May94   **Width is approx. 2 miles**

Off US 101, 15 miles south of Gold Beach.

Miner Creek - Samuel H. Boardman SSC

Mgd by:	OPRD
Parking Lot:	**small**
" roadside –	no
Drinking water	no
Tables/benches	no
Restrooms	no
Camping	no
Showers	no
Phone	no
Info Center	no
Fee	no
[Way off the beaten path]	

Nearby Beach Access

Pedestrian	**yes**
Vehicle	**yes**
Boat	no

Recreation

Horse riding	no
Tidepooling	no
WhaleWatching	no
Surfing	no
Bicycling	no
Hiking/trails	no
Boating	no

Rating:

★ ★ ★ ☆ ☆

Fairly steep
and long trail.

This is an
exceptional
place for
photos.

Astoria
Seaside
Tillamook
Lincoln City
Newport
Florence
Reedsport
Coos Bay
Bandon
Port Orford
Gold Beach
Brookings

Aerial photo courtesy of U.S. Geological Survey, 27May94   **Width is approx. 2 miles**

Off US 101, 16 miles south of Gold Beach.

Whaleshead - Samuel H. Boardman SSC

		Nearby Beach Access		Rating:	
Mgd by:	State Parks	Pedestrian	yes	★ ★ ★ ☆ ☆	
Parking Lot:	**medium**	Vehicle	yes		
" roadside –	no	Boat	no	Boardman is	
Drinking water	no			1,471 acres.	
Tables/benches	**yes**	Recreation			
Restrooms	**yes**	Horse riding	no	Has an out-of-	
Camping	no	Tidepooling	**yes**	the-way feel,	
Showers	no	WhaleWatching	no	but definitely is	
Phone	no	Surfing	no	not. You see	
Info Center	no	Bicycling	no	*Whaleshead*	
Fee	no	Hiking/trails	**yes**	both with an 's'	
[No turnaround for RVs]		Boating	no	and not.	

Astoria
Seaside
Tillamook
Lincoln City
Newport
Florence
Reedsport
Coos Bay
Bandon
Port Orford
Gold Beach
Brookings

Road to beach -->

Whaleshead
Island -->

<-- Hwy 101

Aerial photo courtesy of U.S. Geological Survey, 27May94   **Width is approx. 2 miles**

Off US 101, 6½ miles north of Brookings.

Lone Ranch - Samuel H. Boardman SSC

		Nearby Beach Access		Rating:
Mgd by:	State Parks	Pedestrian	**yes**	★ ★ ★ ★ ☆
Parking Lot:	**medium**	Vehicle	**yes**	
" roadside –	**a few**	Boat	no	Boardman is
				1,471 acres.
Drinking water	no			
Tables/benches	**yes**	Recreation		One of the best
Restrooms	**yes**	Horse riding	no	day-use parks
Camping	no	Tidepooling	**yes**	for picnics and
Showers	no	WhaleWatching	no	beach walking.
Phone	no	Surfing	no	
Info Center	no	Bicycling	no	
Fee	no	Hiking/trails	**yes**	
[Scenic, protected cove]		Boating	no	

Astoria
Seaside
Tillamook
Lincoln City
Newport
Florence
Reedsport
Coos Bay
Bandon
Port Orford
Gold Beach
→ Brookings

Cape Ferrelo

Lone Ranch Beach -->

<-- Hwy 101

Twin Rocks

Aerial photo courtesy of U.S. Geological Survey, 27May94   **Width is approx. 2 miles**

North of Brookings 3 miles; Boardman is a 12 linear mile park with waysides.

115

Taylor Creek

Mgd by:	ODOT	Nearby Beach Access		Rating:
Parking Lot:	**small**	Pedestrian	**yes**	★★★☆☆
" roadside –	no	Vehicle	**yes**	
		Boat	no	There are
Drinking water	no			seldom many
Tables/benches	no	Recreation		people here --
Restrooms	no	Horse riding	no	except surfers.
Camping	no	Tidepooling	no	
Showers	no	WhaleWatching	no	
Phone	no	Surfing	**yes**	
Info Center	no	Bicycling	no	
Fee	no	Hiking/trails	**yes**	
[Popular with surfers]		Boating	no	

Astoria
Seaside
Tillamook
Lincoln City
Newport
Florence
Reedsport
Coos Bay
Bandon
Port Orford
Gold Beach
→ Brookings

<-- Hwy 101

Rainbow Island →

Taylor Creek →

White Rock

Aerial photo courtesy of U.S. Geological Survey, 27May94   ***Width is approx. 2 miles***

Off US 101, 1 mile north of Brookings.

Harris Beach State Park

		Nearby Beach Access		Rating:	

Mgd by: State Parks

Parking Lot: **large**

"   roadside –   **yes**

Drinking water   **yes**

Tables/benches   **yes**

Restrooms   **yes**

Camping   **yes**

Showers   **yes**

Phone   **yes**

Info Center   **yes**

Fee (Day use no) **yes**

[Great place to camp]

<u>Nearby Beach Access</u>

Pedestrian   **yes**

Vehicle   **yes**

Boat   no

<u>Recreation</u>

Horse riding   no

Tidepooling   **yes**

WhaleWatching   **yes**

Surfing   **yes**

Bicycling   **yes**

Hiking/trails   **yes**

Boating   no

Rating:

★★★★☆

173 acres.

Oregon's Largest offshore island. Excellent day-use area. Above is a winter scene.

Astoria
Seaside
Tillamook
Lincoln City
Newport
Florence
Reedsport
Coos Bay
Bandon
Port Orford
Gold Beach
→ Brookings

Aerial photo courtesy of U.S. Geological Survey, 27May94   ***Width is approx. 2 miles***

Off US 101, on the north edge of Brookings.

Sport Haven Park

Mgd by: Port of Brookings		Nearby Beach Access		Rating:		Astoria
Parking Lot:	**large**	Pedestrian	**yes**	★★★☆☆		Seaside
" roadside –	**yes**	Vehicle	**yes**			
		Boat	**yes**	Many activities		Tillamook
Drinking water	**yes**			in the harbor		Lincoln City
Tables/benches	**yes**	Recreation		area: stores,		Newport
Restrooms	**yes**	Horse riding	no	motel,		
Camping	no	Tidepooling	no	restaurants,		Florence
Showers	no	WhaleWatching	no	locally caught		Reedsport
Phone	**yes**	Surfing	**yes**	and canned		Coos Bay
Info Center	no	Bicycling	no	tuna and		Bandon
Fee	no	Hiking/trails	no	salmon.		Port Orford
[A large RV park is here]		Boating	**nearby**			Gold Beach
					→	Brookings

Aerial photo courtesy of U.S. Geological Survey, 27May94   ***Width is approx. 2 miles***

In the Port of Brookings harbor.

McVay Rock State Recreation Site

					Rating:
Mgd by:	State Parks	**Nearby Beach Access**			
Parking Lot:	**small**	Pedestrian	**yes**		★★★☆☆
" roadside –	no	Vehicle	**yes**		
		Boat	no		Maintained
Drinking water	no				well by local
Tables/benches	no	**Recreation**			residents. Has
Restrooms	no	Horse riding	no		a large grassy
Camping	no	Tidepooling	**yes**		area on top of
Showers	no	WhaleWatching	**yes**		the bluff that
Phone	no	Surfing	no		used to be a
Info Center	no	Bicycling	no		lily field.
Fee	no	Hiking/trails	no		
[Popular dog exercise area]		Boating	no		

Astoria
Seaside
Tillamook
Lincoln City
Newport
Florence
Reedsport
Coos Bay
Bandon
Port Orford
Gold Beach
Brookings

McVay Rock SRS –>

<– Hwy 101

Oceanview Dr –>

Aerial photo courtesy of U.S. Geological Survey, 27May94   **Width is approx. 2 miles**

Off US 101, 2 miles south of Brookings on Oceanview Drive.

Winchuck State Recreation Site

Mgd by: State Parks		Nearby Beach Access		Rating:	
Parking Lot:	**large**	Pedestrian	**yes**	★★☆☆☆	Astoria
" roadside –	**a few**	Vehicle	**yes**		Seaside
		Boat	possibly	Path to ocean	Tillamook
Drinking water	no			sometimes is	Lincoln City
Tables/benches	no	Recreation		washed out.	Newport
Restrooms	no	Horse riding	no		Florence
Camping	no	Tidepooling	no	Crissey Airfield	Reedsport
Showers	no	WhaleWatching	no	SRS on south	Coos Bay
Phone	no	Surfing	no	side is better;	Bandon
Info Center	no	Bicycling	no	only road-side	Port Orford
Fee	no	Hiking/trails	no	parking there,	Gold Beach
[Fishing, clams, dog walking]		Boating	no	however.	Brookings

Aerial photo courtesy of U.S. Geological Survey, 27May94   ***Width is approx. 2 miles***

On the north side of the US 101 bridge over the Winchuck River.

Crissey Field State Recreation Site

		Nearby Beach Access		Rating:	
Mgd by:	State Parks	Pedestrian	**yes**	★★★☆☆	
Parking Lot:	no	Vehicle	**yes**		
" roadside –	**a few**	Boat	no	500 yards to	
Drinking water	no			the beach on a	
Tables/benches	no	Recreation		good trail.	
Restrooms	no	Horse riding	**yes**	Recently was	
Camping	no	Tidepooling	no	named a state	
Showers	no	WhaleWatching	no	park a/c an-	
Phone	no	Surfing	no	other visitor	
Info Center	no	Bicycling	no	center may be	
Fee	no	Hiking/trails	no	built here. Was	
[Completely undeveloped]		Boating	no	WW II airfield.	

Astoria
Seaside
Tillamook
Lincoln City
Newport
Florence
Reedsport
Coos Bay
Bandon
Port Orford
Gold Beach
Brookings

Crissey Field SRS -->

Winchuck River

Oregon - California border

<-- Hwy 101

Aerial photo courtesy of U.S. Geological Survey, 27May94   **Width is approx. 2 miles**

South side of the US 101 bridge over the Winchuck River. On border w/California.

APPENDIX

Where To Find Things (in north to south order)

Drinking Water
Fort Stevens - 1
Indian Beach - 4
Crescent Beach - 5
Cannon Beach - 6
Tolovanna Beach - 7
Short Sand Beach - 12
Nehalem Bay -14
Manhattan Beach -16
Barview Jetty Co. Park - 18
Cape Meares - 21
Cape Lookout - 25
Bob Straub - 28
Roads End - 31
Wecoma Beach - 32
D River - 33
Schooner Creek - 34
Siletz Bay Park - 35
Gleneden Beach - 36
Fogarty Creek - 38
Devil's Punch Bowl - 39
Beverly Beach - 40
Agate Beach - 44
Nye Beach - 45
Yaquina Bay - 46
South Beach - 47
Lost Creek - 48
Ona Beach - 49
Seal Rock - 51
Driftwood Beach - 53
Beachside - 58
Tillicum Beach - 59
Yachats - 62
Devil's Churn - 64
Cummins Creek - 67
Carl G. Washburne - 73
Devil's Elbow - 74
Baker Beach - 75
Sutton Creek - 76
South Jetty ODNRA - 78

Drinking Water (Cont'd)
Jessie M. Honeyman - 79
Siltcoos Beach ODNRA - 80
Umpqua Lighthouse - 82
Horsfall Beach - 83
Sunset Bay - 85
Shore Acres - 86
Bullards Beach - 90
Face Rock - 93
Cape Blanco - 95
Battle Rock - 98
Humbug Mountain - 100
Ophir Beach - 102
Harris Beach - 117
Sport Haven - 118

Tables/benches
Fort Stevens - 1
Indian Beach - 4
Crescent Beach - 5
Cannon Beach - 6
Tolovanna Beach - 7
Arcadia Beach - 8
Hug Point - 9
Short Sand Beach - 12
Nehalem Bay - 14
Manhattan Beach - 16
Barview Jetty Co. Park - 18
Cape Meares - 21
Oceanside Beach - 23
Netarts - 24
Cape Lookout - 25
Cape Kiwanda Launch - 27
Bob Straub - 28
Roads End - 31
Wecoma Beach - 32
D River - 33
Schooner Creek - 34
Siletz Bay Park - 35
Gleneden Beach - 36

Tables/benches (Cont'd)
Fogarty Creek - 38
Devil's Punch Bowl - 39
Beverly Beach - 40
Agate Beach - 44
Nye Beach -45
Yaquina Bay - 46
South Beach - 47
Lost Creek - 48
Ona Beach - 49
Seal Rock - 51
Driftwood Beach - 53
William P. Keady - 54
Governor Patterson - 55
Beachside - 58
Tillicum Beach - 59
Smelt Sands - 61
Yachats - 62
Yachats Ocean Road - 63
Devil's Churn - 64
Cook's Chasm - 66
Cummins Creek - 67
Strawberry Hill - 68
Bob Creek - 69
Ocean Beach - 71
Muriel O. Ponsler - 72
Carl G. Washburne - 73
Devil's Elbow - 74
Baker Beach - 75
Sutton Creek - 76
Jessie M. Honeyman - 79
Siltcoos Beach - 80
Umpqua Lighthouse - 82
Sunset Bay - 85
Shore Acres - 86
Cape Arago - 87
Seven Devils - 88
Whiskey Run - 89
Bullards Beach - 90
Face Rock - 93
Beach Loop Drive - 94
Cape Blanco - 95
Agate Beach - 97
Battle Rock - 98
Humbug Mountain - 100
Ophir Beach - 102

Tables/benches (Cont'd)
Curry Co. South Beach - 107
Pistol River - 111
Arch Rock - 112
Whaleshead - 114
Lone Ranch - 115
Harris Beach - 117
Sport Haven - 118

Restrooms
Fort Stevens - 1
Indian Beach - 4
Crescent Beach - 5
Cannon Beach - 6
Tolovanna Beach - 7
Arcadia Bach - 8
Hug Point - 9
Short Sand Beach -12
Nehalem Bay - 14
Manhattan Beach - 16
Barview Jetty Co. Park - 18
Cape Meares - 21
Oceanside Beach - 23
Netarts - 24
Cape Lookout - 25
Cape Kiwanda Launch - 27
Bob Straub - 28
Neskowin Beach - 29
Cascade Head/Knight Park - 30
Roads End - 31
Wecoma Beach - 32
D River - 33
Schooner Creek - 34
Siletz Bay Park - 35
Gleneden Beach - 36
Fogarty Creek - 38
Devil's Punch Bowl - 39
Beverly Beach - 40
Yaquina Head - 43
Agate Beach - 44
Nye Beach - 45
Yaquina Bay - 46
South Beach - 47
Lost Creek - 48
Ona Beach - 49
Seal Rock - 51

Restrooms (Cont'd)

Driftwood Beach - 53
William P. Keady - 54
Governor Patterson - 55
Beachside - 58
Tillicum Beach - 59
Smelt Sands - 61
Yachats - 62
Yachats Ocean Road - 63
Devils Churn - 64
Cummins Creek - 67
Strawberry Hill - 68
Bob Creek - 69
Ocean Beach - 71
Carl G. Washburne - 73
Devil's Elbow - 74
Baker Beach - 75
Sutton Creek - 76
Siuslaw North Jetty - 77
South Jetty Road ODNRA - 78
Jessie M. Honeyman - 79
Siltcoos Beach - 80
Umpqua Lighthouse - 82
Horsfall Beach - 83
Bastendorf Beach - 84
Sunset Bay - 85
Shore Acres - 86
Cape Arago - 87
Seven Devils - 88
Whiskey Run - 89
Bullards Beach - 90
Coquille River Lighthouse - 91
South Jetty Co. Park - 92
Face Rock - 93
Beach Loop Drive - 94
Cape Blanco - 95
Agate Beach - 97
Battle Rock - 98
Humbug Mountain - 100
Ophir Beach - 102
South Jetty Rogue River - 106
Curry Co. Fairgrounds - 107
Cape Sebastian - 109
Pistol River - 111
Arch Rock - 112
Whaleshead - 114

Restrooms (Cont'd)

Lone Ranch - 115
Harris Beach - 117
Sport Haven - 118

Camping

Fort Stevens - 1
Indian Beach - 4
Short Sand Beach - 12
Nehalem Bay - 14
Barview Jetty Co. Park - 18
Cape Lookout - 25
Beverly Beach - 40
South Beach - 47
Beachside - 58
Tillicum Beach - 59
Carl G. Washburne - 73
Baker Beach - 75
Sutton Creek - 76
Jessie M. Honeyman - 79
Siltcoos Beach - 80
Umpqua Lighthouse - 82
Horsfall Beach - 83
Sunset Bay - 85
Bullards Beach - 90
Cape Blanco - 95
Humbug Mountain - 100
Harris Beach - 117

Showers

Fort Stevens - 1
Nehalem Bay - 14
Barview Jetty Co. Park - 18
Cape Lookout - 25
Beverly Beach - 40
South Beach - 47
Beachside - 58
Jessie M. Honeyman - 79
Umpqua Lighthouse - 82
Sunset Bay 85
Bullards Beach - 90
Cape Blanco - 95
Humbug Mountain - 100
Harris Beach - 117

Phone
Fort Stevens - 1
Crescent Beach - 5
Cannon Beach - 6
Tolovanna Beach - 7
Short Sand Beach - 12
Nehalem Bay -14
Barview Jetty Co. Park - 18
Cape Lookout - 25
Beverly Beach - 40
South Beach - 47
Beachside - 58
Devil's Churn - 64
Jessie M. Honeyman - 79
Umpqua Lighthouse - 82
Horsfall Beach - 83
Humbug Mountain - 100
Ophir Beach - 102
Harris Beach - 117
Sport Haven - 118

Info Center
Fort Stevens - 1
Tolovanna Beach - 7
Nehalem Bay - 14
Barview Jetty Co. Park - 18
Cape Meares - 21
Cape Lookout - 25
Siletz Bay Park - 35
Devil's Punch Bowl - 39
Beverly Beach - 40
Yaquina Head - 43
Yaquina Bay - 46
South Beach - 47
Seal Rock - 51
Beachside - 58
Devil's Churn - 64
Cook's Chasm - 66
Jessie M. Honeyman - 79
Sunset Bay - 85
Shore Acres - 86
Bullards Beach - 90
Humbug Mountain - 100
Harris Beach - 117

Fee
Fort Stevens - 1
Indian Beach - 4
Crescent Beach - 5
Barview Jetty Co. Park - 18
Cape Lookout - 25
Fogarty Creek - 38
Yaquina Head - 43
South Beach - 47
Tillicum Beach - 59
Devil's Churn - 64
Cape Cove - 65
Devil's Elbow - 74
Baker Beach - 75
Sutton Creek - 76
South Jetty Road ODNRA - 78
Jessie M. Honeyman - 79
Siltcoos Beach - 80
Umpqua Lighthouse - 82
Sunset Bay - 85
Shore Acres - 86
Bullards Beach - 90
Cape Blanco - 95
Humbug Mountain - 100

Lighthouses
Tillamook Rock - 4, 5
Cape Meares* - 21
Yaquina Head* - 43
Yaquina Bay* - 46
Heceta Head* - 74
Umpqua* - 82
Cape Arago - 87
Coquille River* - 91
Cape Blanco* - 95
*Can be toured

Horse Riding
Fort Stevens - 1
Del Rey Beach - 3
Cannon Beach - 6
Neahkahnie Beach - 13
Nehalem Bay - 14
Bay Ocean Spit - 19
Cape Kiwanda Launch - 27
Bob Straub - 28

Horse Riding (Cont'd)
Neskowin Beach - 29
Baker Beach - 75
Horsfall Beach - 83
Bullards Beach - 90
Face Rock - 93
Cape Blanco - 95
Doyle Point - 105
South Jetty Rogue River - 106
Curry Co. Fairgrounds - 107
Pistol River - 111
Crissey Field - 120

Tidepooling
Indian Beach - 4
Crescent Beach - 5
Cannon Beach - 6
Short Sand Beach - 12
Cape Lookout - 25
Cape Kiwanda SNA - 26
Cape Kiwanda Launch - 27
Fogarty Creek - 38
Devil's Punch Bowl - 39
Yaquina Head - 43
Seal Rock - 51
Smelt Sands - 61
Yachats - 62
Yachats Ocean Road - 63
Devil's Churn - 64
Cape Cove - 65
Cook's Chasm - 66
Cummins Creek - 67
Strawberry Hill - 68
Bob Creek -69
Carl G. Washburne - 73
Sunset Bay - 85
Cape Arago - 87
Face Rock - 93
Beach Loop Drive - 94
Cape Blanco - 95
Whaleshead - 114
Lone Ranch - 115
Harris Beach - 117
McVay Rock - 119

WhaleWatching
Fort Stevens - 1
Crescent Beach - 5
Cove Beach - 11
Short Sand Beach - 12
Neahkahnie Beach - 13
Nehalem Bay - 14
Cape Meares - 21
Cape Lookout - 25
Cape Kiwanda SNA - 26
Cape Kiwanda Launch - 27
D River - 33
Devil's Punch Bowl - 39
Beverly Beach - 40
Moolack Beach - 42
Yaquina Head - 43
Yaquina Bay - 46
Seal Rock - 51
Yachats - 62
Yachats Ocean Road - 63
Devil's Churn - 64
Cape Cove - 65
Cook's Chasm - 66
Strawberry Hill - 68
Carl G. Washburne - 73
Heceta Head Lighthouse - 74
Umpqua Lighthouse - 82
Shore Acres - 86
Cape Arago - 87
Face Rock - 93
Cape Blanco - 95
Battle Rock - 98
Cape Sebastian - 109
Harris Beach - 117
McVay Rock - 119

Surfing
Fort Stevens - 1
Del Rey Beach - 3
Indian Beach - 4
Short Sand Beach - 12
Neahkahnie Beach - 13
Nehalem Bay - 14
Oceanside Beach - 23
Cape Kiwanda SNA - 26
Cape Kiwanda Launch - 27

Surfing (Cont'd)

Roads End - 31
D River - 33
Schooner Creek - 34
Gleneden Beach - 36
Devil's Punch Bowl - 39
Beverly Beach - 40
Moolack Beach - 42
Yaquina Head - 43
Agate Beach - 44
Yaquina Bay - 46
South Beach - 47
Ona Beach - 49
Muriel O. Ponsler - 72
South Jetty ODNRA - 78
Sparrow Park - 81
Bastendorf Beach - 84
Sunset Bay - 85
Seven Devils - 88
Whiskey Run - 89
Battle Rock - 98
Hubbard Creek - 99
Pistol River - 111
Taylor Creek - 116
Harris Beach - 117
Sport Haven - 118

Bicycling

Fort Stevens - 1
Cannon Beach - 6
Neahkahnie Beach - 13
Nehalem Bay - 14
Bay Ocean - 19
Cape Lookout - 25
Neskowin Beach - 29
Cascade Head - 30
South Beach - 47
Cook's Chasm - 66
Cummins Creek - 67
Sutton Creek - 76
Jessie M. Honeyman - 79
Sunset Bay - 85
Seven Devils - 88
Whiskey Run - 89
Bullards Beach - 90
Humbug Mountain - 100
Harris Beach - 117

Hiking/trails

Fort Stevens - 1
Indian Beach - 4
Crescent Beach - 5
Arch Cape - 10
Cove Beach - 11
Short Sand Beach - 12
Nehalem Bay - 14
Barview Jetty Co. Park - 18
Bay Ocean Spit - 19
Cape Meares - 21
Cape Lookout - 25
Cape Kiwanda SNA - 26
Cape Kiwanda Launch - 27
Cascade Head - 30
Fogarty Creek - 38
Devil's Punch Bowl - 39
Beverly Beach - 40
Yaquina Head - 43
Yaquina Bay - 46
South Beach - 47
Seal Rock - 51
Governor Patterson - 55
Beachside - 58
Smelt Sands - 61
Devil's Churn - 64
Cape Cove Marine Gardens - 65
Cook's Chasm - 66
Cummins Creek - 67
Bob Creek - 69
Muriel O. Ponsler - 72
Carl G. Washburne - 73
Devil's Elbow - 74
Baker Beach - 75
Sutton Creek - 76
Jessie M. Honeyman - 79
Siltcoos Beach - 80
Sparrow Park - 81
Umpqua Lighthouse - 82
Horsfall Beach - 83
Sunset Bay - 85
Shore Acres - 86
Cape Arago - 87
Seven Devils - 88
Whiskey Run - 89
Bullards Beach - 90
Face Rock - 93

Hiking/trails (Cont'd)
Beach Loop Drive - 94
Cape Blanco - 95
Battle Rock - 98
Humbug Mountain - 100
Cape Sebastian - 109
Pistol River - 111
Whaleshead - 114
Lone Ranch - 115
Taylor Creek - 116
Harris Beach - 117

Boating
Fort Stevens - 1
Nehalem Bay - 14
Netarts - 24
Cape Lookout - 25
Cape Kiwanda SNA - 26
Cape Kiwanda Launch - 27
Bob Straub - 28
Cascade Head - 30
South Beach - 47
Ona Beach - 49
Sutton Creek - 76
Jessie M. Honeyman - 79
Siltcoos Beach - 80
Umpqua Lighthouse - 82
Sunset Bay - 85
Bullards Beach - 90
Cape Blanco - 95
South Jetty Rogue River - 106
Sport Haven - 118

INDEX

Pistol River SSV - 111
Roads End SRS - 31
Schooner Creek - 34
Seal Rock SRS - 51
Seven Devils SRS - 88
Shore Acres State Park - 86
Short Beach at Cape Meares - 22
Short Sand Beach - 12
Siletz Bay Park - 35
Siltcoos Beach - ODNRA - 80
Siuslaw River North Jetty - 77
Smelt Sands State Park - 61
South Beach State Park - 47
South Jetty County Park - 92
South Jetty Rd, ODNRA - 78
South Jetty Rogue River - 106
Sparrow Park - ODNRA - 81
Sport Haven Park - 118
Stonefield Beach SRS - 70
Strawberry Hill, Neptune SSV - 68
Sunset Bay State Park - 85
Sunset Beach - 2
Sutton Creek Recreation Area - 76
Taylor Creek - 116
Tillicum Beach Campground - 59
Tolovanna Beach SRS - 7
Twin Rocks - 17
Umpqua Lighthouse SP - 82
Vingie Lane, Yachats - 60
Wade Creek - 41
Wecoma Beach - 32
Whaleshead - 114
Whiskey Run, Seven Devils - 89
Winchuck River Wayside - 120
Wm. Keady Wayside - 54
Yachats SRA - 62
Yachats Ocean Road SNA - 63
Yaquina Bay SRA - 46
Yaquina Head - 43